H-G FEB 3 '97

Sammy Davis Jr.

Tracey Davis

with Dolores A. Barclay

GPG

General Publishing Group, Inc.
Los Angeles

Publisher: W. Quay Hays
Managing Editor: Peter L. Hoffman
Art Director: Maritta Tapanainen
Projects Manager: Trudihope Schlomowitz
Production Director: Nadeen Torio
Color and Pre-Press Manager: Bill Castillo
Color and Pre-Press Director: Gaston Moraga
Production Assistants: Tom Archibeque, Alan Peak

Photo Credits, Back Cover: Left, The Rothman Collection; Middle, photo
    by Bernie Abramson, courtesy The Rothman Collection; Right, The
    Davis Family Collection

For information:

General Publishing Group, Inc.
2701 Ocean Park Blvd., Ste. 140
Santa Monica, CA 90405

Library of Congress Cataloging-in-Publication Data

Davis, Tracey
    Sammy Davis Jr., my father / by Tracey Davis with Dolores A. Barclay.
        p.   cm.
    Includes index.
    ISBN 1-881649-84-9
    1. Davis, Sammy, 1925-1990. 2. Davis, Tracey. 3. Entertainers--United
States--Biography. 4. Children of entertainers--United States--
Biography. I. Barclay, Dolores A. II. Title.
PN2287.D322D38   1996
792.7'028'092--dc20
    [B]   96-2531
                                                                       CIP

Printed in the USA
10 9 8 7 6 5 4 3 2 1

General Publishing Group
Los Angeles

Dedication

Julie Clark,
thanks for insisting that
I open a dialogue with my father.
You did the impossible,
you gave me my father back.

To the Millers
in Red Bluff, California.
Thanks for screwing my head on right
and reaffirming to me
just what is important in life.
I love you all.

Acknowledgments

Thanks first and foremost to my family: Guy, Sam, Montana. It is cliché to say I couldn't have done it without you, but I couldn't have.

Thanks to my mom for helping me at every turn, whether I wanted your help or not. You are the Best!

Thanks to my brothers Mark and Jeff for opening themselves up and letting me tell the intimate stories of our family.

Thanks to Howard Bennett, the most influential teacher I had at George Whittell High School. You were an inspiration to me during high school, you prepared me for college and for life. You're the best.

Thanks Lessie Lee, the best nanny in the world.

Thanks to my friends Julie Clark, Diane Williams, Andy Hughes, David Hughes and Corby Hughes.

Bernie Abramson, thanks for the wonderful photos of our family and friends and for changing my diapers along the way.

Thanks to Dolores Barclay for being "in my head."

To Shari, Liliana, Denise, Shelly, thanks for doing my work so I could do this book.

Thank you Don Bellisario, for being the most supportive boss anyone could ask for.

Thank you Cynthia Rawitch, my journalism professor at CSU Northridge and my friend. You gave me the courage to write and proved over and over again you can have it all.

A very special thanks to my agents, Linda Chester and Laurie Fox of the Linda Chester Literary Agency. Thanks for sticking by me and believing in my story.

To Dana, thanks for being the sister I never had.

To my godchildren, Taryn, Lauren and Jeff. I love you.

For you, Pop

Chapter One

I was plowing through a field of mud, going nowhere fast. The soft mass sucked at my shoes and shackled my legs. I couldn't move. I was stuck. My muscles howled in pain, but I had to keep moving. And so I willed myself forward another inch. The mud clung to me even more, dragging me down, down, down.

I screamed.

I woke up!

I hate dreams like that, and lately I'd been having too many of them. They were tense projections of a gnawing feeling that something was going to happen—something that would change my life forever. No, it wasn't my upcoming wedding to Guy Garner. It was a feeling centered around Dad. For some time I had wanted to talk to him about our relationship, but I didn't know how to go about doing it. After all, you just don't call up the great Sammy Davis Jr. and say, "By the way, you're a lousy father." I didn't have the nerve, and I didn't even know where to begin. I had a laundry list of wrongs and my resentment toward my father had mushroomed into something dark and distasteful.

It was 1986, I was 25 years old and I felt frustrated and incomplete as far as my relationship with my father went. Every time I tried to sort through my feelings, my father's image surfaced and wouldn't shake loose. Talking to Dad was the key. If I was ever to grasp any understanding of myself and move on in my life, I had to settle up with Pop. But it wasn't that easy. Just the thought of a confrontation brought on a cold sweat and a mild bout of hyperventilation. I was terrified of talking to my own father about anything important. He always wanted to know the bottom line—not the reasons for something, just the outcome.

With my wedding fast approaching, my mind was on other matters. But my conflicts with Dad danced beneath the surface, ruffling my good cheer.

Mom and my good friend Julie Clark kept asking me about a bridal shower, and I kept telling them I'd kill anyone who gave me one. I always hated those things. They reminded me of Tupperware parties, only with my friends, someone was more likely to wrap up a basket full of flavored condoms than an electric can opener. So I got out of bed and called Julie, my maid of honor, who would be the person to organize a party for me.

"I know you guys are cooking up something, but *don't.* I don't want the ribbon hat, I don't want the crepe paper umbrella, I don't want lacy lingerie I'll never wear or three dozen can openers," I said.

"Come on, Trace. I know you hate showers, but we can do something different—we can have a party at the beach and have some margs," Julie said.

"Yahoo. Now you're talking," I said.

We were on the phone for a while and all the time I kept thinking about how much I wanted to make this celebration different. I wanted to do something cool, something big. Guy and his pals were having a stag party and a wild night on the town. I wasn't into that. What I wanted was to do something where we—and especially me—could be pampered, spend money, relax.

Then an idea slammed into me and I told Julie I'd call her back. I hung up the phone and quickly called information for the number of the Desert Inn Casino in Las Vegas. I managed to get Murphy Bennett, my father's longtime assistant, on the phone and got through to my father. Murphy had been with Dad longer than I had been alive—

through the early days of Dad's solo act, through the Civil Rights Movement and marches with Martin Luther King Jr.

"Hey, Pop, how are ya? I'm great, too." Pop was in a terrific mood. The wedding had him excited.

"Anyway, the reason I'm calling—me and Jules want to come and hang out with you. Kind of a pre-wedding wild weekend."

"Oh, yeah, Julie Clark," Pop said. Julie was one of the few friends of mine Dad absolutely loved.

"Well, I thought it would be great if she and I came over there for the weekend and hung out and just had a little fun, sort of like a bachelor party, but just me and Jules."

"Sure. Great. Come on up," Pop said. "You guys can take the upstairs of my suite."

I hung up, redialed and exploded on the phone with Julie. "Vegas. No shit. Dad's going to be doing a show at the Desert Inn. We can hang out at Bally's—there's a great spa there."

"Cool. I'm already packed." Julie was fast.

On the drive out, I couldn't shake the feeling that something important was going to happen. I was on edge and I kept thinking about Dad. There was this sense of needing to dig below the surface and figure things out. I confessed my feelings to my friend, who understood me better than anyone else. Julie knew the relationship between me and Dad had never been great, and she'd always encouraged me to try harder and communicate my feelings, to make things right before it was too late.

"You know, I wish I could talk to him," I said, keeping a steady 75 on the desert drive. "I love him, Jules, I really do. I know he cares, but he doesn't really know me. You know how much it bugs me that he never calls me himself, that he always has someone else do it."

"I know," Julie said.

"Julie. He doesn't know my phone number," I said.

We were both silent for a while. I could tell Julie was turning something over in her mind. I welcomed the silence because I didn't want any lectures right then. But

Julie doesn't give up easily—that's why she's such a good friend. She turned to me and said, "Trace, when my Dad left us, I still had all these unresolved feelings and issues. I never had a chance to tell him how I really feel and he still doesn't know all my good intentions. You should talk to your father *now*—before he gets old and dies. You love him and he loves you."

I knew she was right but I couldn't bring myself to do it.

"Jules, I'm too much of a wuss. I can't do it, man. I can't confront *Sammy Davis Jr.* God, that's going to be the hardest thing I've ever done in my life. Talking to my father."

"Do it," she said gently. "He loves you."

"I know that," I said. Or did I? I wasn't sure about anything anymore. I just knew our whole relationship and everything from the past was haunting me. I don't know why it all surfaced at that precise point in time. Maybe it just had been brewing in some giant emotional cauldron since I was a little girl. Or maybe that's what the prospect of marriage does, forces us to smear our lives on a microscope slide and probe every tiny detail. Whatever the reason, it was real and it wasn't going anywhere.

But I also knew how strange and out of place I felt about talking to my father about anything intimate. I had no idea how to do it. If you see a close friend with spinach on his teeth, you tell him—because you're close and you can say anything. With my mom, I never held back. I could turn to her and say, "Gosh, Mom, that sweater looks terrible. You should change into another one," and the world wouldn't explode. But if I criticized Dad, it might prove a fatal blow for the planet. He could banish me from his life and I might not ever be able to get back in. I always thought it was better to be superficially included than to be totally shut out.

It wasn't my place to say anything to my father except chit chat—never get into anything deep, anything that implied a commitment. I was Sammy's Kid, but he was the only person in the world who didn't know it.

Julie wouldn't give up, and the ride to Vegas grew increasingly uncomfortable. The more I thought about talking to Pop, the more my stomach churned. By the time we pulled into the drive at the Desert Inn, I was a nervous wreck. And Julie had convinced me that talking to my father was the right thing to do. It was funny, I thought: I'm in the gambling capital of the world and if there was a place to gamble on our entire relationship, this would be it.

I called Dad right away, and he had started his preshow routine: an early dinner, bath, getting dressed. Jules and I settled into our upstairs suite and told Dad we'd hang backstage that night. We had hours to ourselves. No problem. Off to the gym, then intense lounging and serious kicking back at the pool. Afterward, we looked like total slimeballs—no makeup, scary hair, sweat, oil.

We slunk back to the room to shower and change. I stepped into a pair of cream-colored slacks and a matching V-neck sweater, while Julie went more upscale and young professional with a simple Calvin Klein sleeveless shift and jacket. She looked gorgeous, even though she fretted about not wearing pantyhose. I guess it's her Midwestern attitude.

When we got to Dad's dressing room before the show, Julie began to drop hints about the importance of talking, of communicating. Poor Pop didn't have a clue what we were chattering about.

Then Julie stunned me by turning to Dad and saying, "Mr. Davis, I love you very much. I just had to tell you that because I've always felt close to you. I guess I always feel close to my friends' fathers because I wasn't very close to my own dad."

Tears threatened to spill from Julie's brimming eyes and, as emotionally revved up as I had been all day, I was about to cry as well. But Pop in his over-the-top way cut through the gushy stuff and said, "Oh, come on! I got a show to do. Now scram."

We both smiled and giggled like six-year-olds and sped down the hallway to sit out front.

The 700-seat showroom at the Desert Inn was jammed and the audience primed, like someone had infused 100 volts into everyone's seat. Dad always attracted enthusiastic crowds. He also drew A-list celebrities. Eddie Murphy and 10,000 of his closest friends sat at a table up front near the stage. Eddie always loved to travel with an entourage, and that night was no exception. I looked at him and smiled, remembering how people used to talk about Pop and his huge following. But really, it was just friends hanging out and sometimes the circle grew.

Dad sprinted out like a 20-year-old, and we all felt a charge of electricity shoot through the room. There was a great excitement, the tingling type of exhilaration that makes goose bumps swell on your arms. I looked around and saw wall-to-wall smiles. God, they loved him! We were all experiencing the same thing, that special marriage between a great performer and his willing subjects. Dad was always good; after all, he was the consummate professional. But that night, he was outrageous! He was reaching people in every corner of the room, touching them in places only they knew. His voice carried a power and commitment I'd heard only a few times before. He was on, really on.

He performed some special songs that night. One he dedicated to Julie because he knew how much she liked it. It was "And I Am Telling You I'm Not Going," that gut-jabbing gospel ballad from *Dreamgirls*. Dad didn't just sing it, he spent time telling the audience about the musical and setting up the story. By the time he crooned the first note, he had them sitting on the edge of their seats.

When he finished, the applause came in waves, reached a peak and threatened to remain there. Dad quieted down everyone by saying, "That was for my daughter's friend Jules." Then he introduced the celebrities in the audience. He called Eddie Murphy's name; Eddie grinned from ear to ear and said something only Dad could hear. Then Dad looked at me and said, "With your kind permission, I'd like to take the pleasure of introducing my daughter, Tracey. She's going to be married next week. So let's all wish her well. Please stand up, Trace." I thought I'd die of embarrassment. I was never very good at those public things, Sammy's Kid or not.

It was so sweet, though. Then Pop did something just as nice—he performed a song especially for me. It's my favorite Sammy Davis Jr. song: It was written by a guy who lives in London, but Dad had never recorded the tune, although he wanted to. I never really knew the title, but it's a beautiful ballad about the good times and bad times of a singer. "If I never sing another song or take another bow, I would get by but I don't know how...." I listened to those words, and what I love about that song is that the lyrics tell the story of Sammy Davis Jr. I think that's why Pop loved it, too.

The song made me a little sad, but I didn't really start to cry until Dad sang "Mr. Bojangles." I always hated when Dad performed that tune because there's something so melancholic about the lyrics and the melody. It's a song of such...foreboding. Even Dad thought so. He used to say he hoped he would never end up like the song's Bojangles, a washed-up singer dancing for coins on the street in baggy pants and worn-out shoes. But his rendition of "Mr. Bojangles" was such a dramatic moment. He whistled the final chords, bathed in a single, lonely spotlight with derby cocked on his head.

Dad came back for an encore and polished off the remainder of the set with some of Frank Sinatra's trademark songs. It happened that Frank, Dad's best friend, was performing down the street at the Golden Nugget. The audience loved this tribute to Frank, and so did we.

After the show, Julie and I raced back to Dad's dressing room. A few people stopped by, including Eddie Murphy.

"Hey, baby, glad you could come," Dad said, giving Eddie a hug. "I'd like you to meet my daughter, Tracey, and her friend Julie. They have their Eddie Murphy outfits on. Man, you should have seen them earlier. Whew! But they clean up well."

Eddie howled, and Julie and I felt like falling through the floor. Pop cracked up and then we did, too.

"Gotta run, man. Thank you, you were great," Eddie said as he made room for another well-wisher.

Then Pop turned to us. "So, my dears, what devilment

have you planned for the evening?"

"I dunno, we just sort of thought we'd hang out somewhere," I answered.

"No plans. Good. Then you're both coming with me to catch Frank. OK?" Julie was already halfway to the limo as we all galloped through the kitchen and service entrance to Dad's car. Pop's usual security guys were right by our sides, guns in holsters.

Of all the times I'd spent in Las Vegas with my father, none was as special as the ride that night from the Desert Inn to the Nugget. During that ride I made the decision to talk to my father about our relationship. Just making the commitment to do so made me feel light-headed, a little floaty and very, very frightened. You had to gear up for this kind of talk with Sammy Davis Jr.

I rolled down the window and gulped in some of the hot night air, knowing this talk was going to be difficult for me. But I tried to untangle my nerves and enjoy the trip. This was, after all, my bridal shower!

The car pulled into the parking lot and cruised to the service entrance. How ironic. When Pop first played in Las Vegas, he was forced to enter casinos through the kitchen because he was black. Now he did so because he was a superstar and needed to avoid crazy crowds! It was my father, Sammy Davis Jr., who'd made the casino owners integrate. He'd refused to perform if blacks were refused entry; he'd also refused to perform if he, his father and "Uncle" Will Mastin—the Will Mastin Trio—couldn't also stay in the casino and use the restaurants, bars and gaming rooms. And it wasn't just Las Vegas where Dad made his stand, it was everywhere he went: the Copacabana in New York; Miami Beach, where, in the 1950s and 1960s, Pop and all black people had to carry passes in order to travel at night; Chicago; Cleveland; and Washington, D.C.

I considered all that as casino security men and Dad's personal bodyguard carved a path for us through the steaming, stainless-steel kitchen of the Nugget.

The Nugget was Frank's place. He had a lock on that

casino, just as Dad did at the Desert Inn and Caesars Palace. And Frank's fans were just as fierce as Dad's. Frank had finished his set by the time we got there, so we went straight to his dressing room.

Frank, like Dad, had a huge bowl of cigarettes—just about every brand imaginable—in the room, as well as baskets and baskets of fresh fruit and a good supply of Dom Perignon. Pictures of his daughters, Tina and Nancy, and other members of his family gave the room a homey look. The delightful Red Buttons was there, as were Phyllis, Christine and Dorothy McGuire, who still had the glow from their recent comeback.

"Hey, Charley (one of Frank's nicknames for Dad), it's too hot in here. Turn up the air," Frank yelled at an air-conditioning guy.

"I think it's just right," Dad said with a smile, because everyone knew how much he loved heat. We all laughed.

"Listen up guys. I have something important to say," Dad said with mock seriousness. "My little girl is getting married." Everyone rushed over to me with kisses and hugs. Frank knew how much I adored champagne, so he uncorked a few bottles. "I wish you much happiness, Tracey," said Frank, who also apologized because he and his wife, Barbara, would be unable to make the wedding. Everyone else echoed the positive sentiment with toasts and good wishes. Pop, of course, had to keep the goofiness going. "Well, you know, she's marrying a white guy," he said. Red Buttons rolled his eyes skyward, clutched his heart and feigned shock. Everyone laughed.

"Hey, Pop, like father, like daughter. You started the trend," I shot back. We howled.

Dad and Frank wrapped their arms around each other and started laughing about the old days, how they had first hooked up and how Frank had helped Dad in the infant days of his solo career.

"This boy came to my dressing room once when I was playing a hole in the wall, and he gave me some advice, and man, was he right," Dad said, giving Frank a warm hug.

"He told me all about being honest with your audience. They know a fake. Baby, you're too much."

From the start, Frank had taken a liking to Dad. He'd paved the way for him at segregated clubs in New York by insisting that management seat him. Later, he helped my father get gigs at those clubs, like the Copa. And when Pop was a star, Frank made sure he got parts in his movies, like *Ocean's Eleven* and *Robin and the Seven Hoods*.

We poured more champagne and everyone began talking at once. Julie kept pinching me and then pulled me over to the side of the room, while Red cracked everyone up about how he'd been in show business for 40 years and "never had a dinner," never been honored for his "contribution." He went on and on until we all laughed ourselves silly.

"Tracey, I can't believe this is happening," Julie said excitedly, almost gulping on the words. "Little Julie Clark from Bryan, Ohio, population 300, having champagne with Frank Sinatra and Sammy Davis Jr. and the McGuire Sisters. Holy shit!"

Phyllis McGuire had wandered over and overheard Julie say she was from Ohio. "Honey, Bryan can't be any smaller than Miamisburg," she said. The McGuire Sisters were born in Miamisburg.

I found all three sisters interesting and really terrific women, but Phyllis intrigued me the most. After all, she had been involved with Sam Giancana, the Chicago Mob boss who was killed in 1975. Phyllis was a hoot that night. She told us about the elaborate security system Giancana had installed in her house: When he was there, he'd push a button so a steel plate would drop down over the windows.

"You know, there was a time when it was fashionable to socialize with the Mob," Dad said. "Everyone did. They were part of Las Vegas."

Pop poured some more champagne into my glass as he laughed with Frank.

I was as light-headed as a goldfish, and I didn't want the night to end. This was my idea of fun—sitting in Frank's dressing room hearing about show biz and just hanging out, with no pressure. But I was with the "elder statesmen" of the business and it was getting late. So Pop, Julie and I said our goodnights, hopped in the limo and headed back to Dad's suite at the Desert Inn for a nightcap.

"Trace, what was it you wanted to talk to your father about?" Julie was at it again.

"Uh, I don't know," I said, hoping she'd just shut up. Dad looked quizzically at both of us and kept saying, "What?" I imagined he just finally thought we were being weird because I was getting married.

The car pulled into the Desert Inn and we walked as a trio, arms linked, to the elevators. As we waited to go up, a group of people came over and they had *that look* in their eyes, that smarmy "Ooooooh, there's Sammy Davis Jr." stare. Pop, feeling particularly fatherly that night, was holding my hand. One hotel guest—a total stranger—elbowed my father and said, "Hey, Sammy, nice woman you got there." Snicker, snicker.

"This is my daughter," Dad said very formally and politely. But I didn't miss the hostility he threw the man. The elevator doors opened and Dad dragged me in just as the creep said, "Yeah, right."

"You fucker," Dad said as the doors closed. He turned to Julie and me. "I apologize for using that language, but I hate people like that. Nothing I could possibly say would make him think that you were my kid." We laughed. Whenever Dad cursed around me, he always said, "Excuse me," not realizing that I had the worst mouth since Lenny Bruce.

We went directly to Dad's suite and Julie began to yawn and mumble something about a bath. She kept winking at me and I knew it was now or never. Dad and I needed to talk and this was it.

"I'll catch you later, Trace. Thanks for everything, Mr. D. This was the night of my life," Julie said.

Her absence left an awkward silence, broken only when Dad went behind the bar. "You want something?" he asked as he busied himself pouring his favorite Strawberry Crush in a glass—a drink he had grown fond of after giving up alcohol about a year or so earlier.

"No. Thank you," I said feebly. My blood felt like it was pumping in stereo, and my stomach began to hurt so badly I thought I had diarrhea. Why was I so nervous about talking to my own father? It was almost like the feeling you get when you sense you're going to be in a car crash and you slam on the brakes and your body turns so hot you can hear it buzz. That's how I felt. I was feverish.

"OK, what is it?" Dad asked sternly.

"Dad, I, ah, ah, I ...."

"What is it, Trace Face? Just *tell* me."

Never in a million years did he think I was going to launch into the discussion of a lifetime. He probably thought I was going to tell him I had financial trouble or was pregnant, because his jaw dropped when I blurted out: "I love you, Pop, but I've never really liked you."

He walked out slowly from behind the bar and stood in front of me, taking a deep drag on his cigarette.

"Yeah, well, I have news for you, Trace. I've never really liked you much, either." He spoke calmly. There was no hostility, but there was a certain amount of reproach. There was no doubt in my mind that he meant each killing word. I also knew, with grave certainty, that I had hurt my father over the years just as much as he had hurt me.

At first, I couldn't respond. I felt stung by what he had said. But I was also so relieved that everything was out in the open. Now we could talk.

When I found my voice, I said, "But Dad, it's your job as a parent to like me no matter what, no matter how bad I am or what I do. That's what parents do."

"Trace Face, I love you more than anything on this earth," he said, and I saw his face begin to fall even more.

"I know you love me, Pop. *But where were you?*"

He walked slowly across the room, never once unlocking his eyes from mine. Then he sat beside me on the sofa, and we journeyed back to my childhood to find out where we both had gone wrong, and to find a way back...together.

Chapter Two

F rankly, I think I chose my parents well. They were the perfect balance: Mom, the little straight arrow, and Dad, the crazy cut-up, both with smiling, enormous hearts.

He was The Entertainer, a black, Puerto Rican, one-eyed Jew whose talented genius made him a hit around the world. She was a Swedish beauty, an actress who was beginning to add stardust to her name. Together they stepped into a world that held them in contempt, a world that refused to accept that they were, after all, just a man and a woman in love.

The courtship of Sammy Davis Jr. and May Britt would hardly cause a blink today, but in 1960 such a union was at best shocking and at worst illegal in certain parts of the United States. It always turns my stomach when I think about what my parents and so many other people had to suffer just to live as human beings. Dad knew what they were letting themselves in for and said as much to my great-grandmother, who helped raise my father. According to Pop, his mother, Elvera, a chorus dancer, chose to go back on the road after he was born and couldn't take care of him. He was left with my great-grandmother, whom Pop called Mama.

But as far as things racial went, Mom didn't have a clue.

From the first moment he saw her, Dad knew he was in love. "Ah, your mother," he told me right before I got married, "she was the love of my life. I knew. I always knew."

Mom, though, was one cool cookie about the whole thing. "Oh, I knew he was interested," she said a while back, "but I just let him pursue me. He was so adorable and so charming."

My mother is a natural. She has a simple, unaffected beauty and an inherent sweetness. Mom was discovered in Italy by Sophia Loren's husband, Carlo Ponti. She came to the United States under contract to 20th Century-Fox. When she was in her early 20s, she married Eddie Gregson, whose family developed all of Thousand Oaks and Westlake, California, and who just about owned half of Los Angeles. But they divorced after a couple of years and remained friends, and Mom continued her movie career. By the time my father met her, she had already made *The Young Lions* and *War and Peace*.

Dad was having lunch one day at the Fox commissary with a young actress named Barbara Luna when a ravishing young blonde walked in. He was consumed by her natural grace, pure beauty and perfectly shaped legs that seemed to stretch a mile. It was my mother, who was starring in a remake of *The Blue Angel*. Barbara Luna was also in the movie. Dad had to meet this glorious blonde. But Sammy Davis Jr. just couldn't walk up to a woman and ask her out on a date. He turned to Barbara Luna for an introduction, but she was reluctant. So Pop threw a party for Dinah Washington after her performance at the Cloisters in Los Angeles and invited May Britt. My mother was so cool that she brought a date to Dad's party! But that didn't stop Dad from calling her again and inviting her over to one of his screening nights. This time, she came alone.

My parents' courtship was as chaste as a Victorian tea party. Dad was truly in love and didn't want to jeopardize their relationship in any way. After all, his life had been threatened a few years earlier for dating another blond actress, Kim Novak.

My mother came from a country that was far more tolerant than the United States. And so she didn't understand why Dad was so reluctant to kiss her in public or hold her hand. Even in New York, he was afraid to take her out to dinner or even lunch—and with good reason. Everywhere my father went, he was dogged by hate mail and bomb threats, and obscene phone callers managed to trail him to his clubs and concert halls. Some theaters in the South refused to play my mother's movies. Pop tried to keep Mom away from his shows because of threats and pickets. But Mom was strong. "Nobody is going to frighten me away from you," she told my father. And no one did.

Those years haunted my father his entire life. I remember how he talked to me and my husband, Guy, who is Italian, about the challenges we would face as a mixed couple. "It's going to be hard," he'd said. "But always remember, it's their problem, not yours. So don't ever let them make it your problem." Once, though, he almost stopped Guy and me when we left the private pool at his suite in Las Vegas and went for a swim in the main pool. "Wow," Dad later said, somewhat startled. "I completely forgot that this is the 1980s, not the 1960s."

He was remembering a time when Lena Horne's daughter jumped into the pool at a Las Vegas hotel and the management drained it after she got out. That type of stuff really scared him. It scared him because he had pushed so hard his entire life to keep me totally unaware of just how harsh the world could be. He could handle it, and I think he knew that I could, too. But he didn't want any ugliness like that in my life, and he worked very hard to eradicate it by committing himself to the Civil Rights Movement.

Dad always credited Harry Belafonte for making him go to Alabama and march with Martin Luther King Jr. My father believed in King and everything he stood for, but he was reluctant to go down to the Deep South in fear for his life. But he did. He went with Marlon Brando and a group of other actors, and they marched with arms linked. Dad said Brando was committed to civil rights but was just as frightened as he was.

I'm proud of my father and my mother, too, for standing up for what they believed in and following their hearts. But even after they got married, they faced an unforgiving and hostile society. People painted obscenities on my parents' garage door and sent them hate mail.

Mom and Dad were married in Dad's house on Nov. 13, 1960, after a month's postponement that came about because of the Kennedys. Through their pal Peter Lawford, who was married to Pat Kennedy, my father and Frank Sinatra got close to the clan and worked tirelessly on John F. Kennedy's campaign. But the fallout from Dad's engagement had an impact on Kennedy's election from the start. At the Democratic convention a few months earlier in August—as my father stood on the stage with Frank, Peter and other celebrities—about five or six delegates from Mississippi booed him. Dad told me about the incident years later, of the humiliation and hurt he felt. Tears welled in his eyes. He said Frank put his hand on his shoulder and the warmth of his friendship helped him through. "Those dirty sons of bitches! Don't let 'em get you," Frank said. But it did get to Dad. Through his tears, he told his buddy, "What did I do to deserve that?"

Frank was Dad's best man. But he kept getting heat in the press and perhaps from the Kennedy camp in its silent, political way that his presence at Dad's wedding would lose votes for John Kennedy. And so my father, to ease things for his friend Frank and to help ensure Kennedy's election, postponed his wedding. The unfortunate part was that, despite everything my father did for Kennedy, he didn't invite him to the Inaugural Ball. Kennedy said it was a concession to Southern politicians. But I call it cowardice. And rudeness. Deep down, though, those were days of hard decisions—each and every day.

But my father loved Bobby Kennedy. He often was invited to Hickory Hill, and when Dad marched with King, Bobby, who was then Attorney General of the United States, sent federal agents to protect my father and the other marchers.

Dad never told Mom the real reason their wedding was postponed. He still was trying to shield her. He suffered the outrage in silence, soothed only by the promise that he and my mother would soon be wed.

The month's delay in my parents' nuptials had one curious side effect: Mom was pregnant with me by the time she got married!

It was early morning, July 5, 1961. My mother slipped into wakefulness. Dad was sitting in a chair by the bed, staring at her.

"I feel something is going to happen," he said in a quiet, serious tone. Mom smiled in that fresh, cherubic way of hers, not knowing that in moments her water would break and she'd begin the pains of childbirth.

It seems I was a demanding little pup from the beginning, deciding to be born right then and there, three weeks before schedule. Mom always said the pillow fight she and Dad had the night before pushed her into an early labor. The fight became a highlight of our family history. By all accounts it had been a spirited night, filled with feathers, giggles and a riot of hugs as my parents chased each other about the house like two frolicking teenagers.

Not only was my world debut far too early, but I was also plunged into the limelight before my time. Pop was one of the biggest names in the country, and Mom was a movie star. That made me a "photo op."

Mom was pretty calm about it all. She knew she had to look good for the press and took her time applying a little makeup before leaving for the hospital. Pop, though, was a basket case; her delay drove him nuts because the labor pains were inching closer and closer together. He was so nervous that he almost ran out of the house in his pajamas. But he didn't forget his camera case! Pop was an accomplished photographer, and he was ready to record the entire event. He insisted on driving Mom himself from our house in the Hollywood Hills to Cedars of Lebanon Hospital. He also took their house guests, Jane and Burt Boyar, who were collaborating with Pop on his autobiography *Yes I Can*.

How surprised they all must have been to hear over the car radio that they were on their way to the hospital for the birth of their first child! Someone at Cedars tipped reporters that Sammy and May would soon be there. Even so, my parents managed to beat the paparazzi, and Pop was able to get Mom safely upstairs without the intrusion of the press. He snapped pictures the whole way, bobbing and weaving around my mother's gurney as it was being rolled into the delivery room. She didn't have long to wait—I arrived almost immediately.

In those days, fathers weren't allowed in the delivery room, which was just as well because my father would not have been able to handle it. Pop was very, very squeamish—

not only couldn't he stand the sight of blood, but he probably would have fainted from seeing everything else expelled from the body during the birth process. So he stayed in a waiting room for fathers making a zillion calls to everyone from my grandfather Sam to Frank Sinatra, who was on the set of his latest movie.

Mom floated in and out of consciousness that day. I was named Tracey Hillevi Davis, for Spencer Tracy (my father adored him) and my grandmother Hillevi in Sweden. After Mom got a peek at me, I was spirited away to the nursery so I could be spruced up for Dad; Mom was carted off to her room to rest.

A nurse rushed off to fetch Pop so he could see me. Another nurse held up my tiny, blanketed form. "A man is not complete until he sees a baby he has made, and by the grace of God I stood there looking at mine, seeing her tiny face and hands, her whole delicate self....I was comfortable in the belief that we were ready to help our child grow up, ready to impart everything we had learned the hard way, able to give her all the love and strength she might need—but I prayed that by the time our baby is grown she would not need all that strength, that she would live in a world of people who would not notice or care about a layer of skin," my Dad wrote in his autobiography.

My father cried and cried, and told whoever was around that I was beautiful.

Dad was awed by the miracle of birth. He couldn't believe he had actually made a child, that the wee being he saw squirming in a blanket was his future. He and Mom truly envisioned an idyllic rainbow family—the three of us, a bold and wonderful testament to the world that color had no meaning.

My mother stayed in the hospital for five days, and Dad was there each day. Finally, it was time to go home. The press, of course, was waiting. Mom flashed her dimples and Pop dazzled with that Sammy Davis Jr. charm as they hurried to the car. Reporters screamed questions and wanted a lot more time than my parents were willing to give. But my father, always gracious, allowed one last question: "What color is the baby?"

He drove away without answering.

Chapter Three

Dad spent 350 days of the year working, mostly on the road, but also in the recording studio and on the movie lot. Still, he managed to stay close to home during the first week of my life. He held a bottle and fed me maybe once or twice, but never ever changed a diaper. As squeamish as he was, just the sight of its contents probably would have pulverized him. I was too little to know or even care who was feeding me or cleaning me, or even if my father was around. Mom was delighted to have him there and enjoy the semblance of a cohesive family. Then, finally, Pop, who had been weaned on nightclubs and vaudeville halls and bars, needed a break from domestic life.

"Frank and Dean asked me to a baseball game," he announced to my mother one day. "Do you mind if I go?" The Brooklyn Dodgers had left New York and now played in Los Angeles and they were the flavor du jour. But Pop, because of work or other career commitments, had never seen a game in its entirety. Mom understood and wanted him to have some fun, so she sent him on his merry way with Frank Sinatra and Dean Martin. I guess Dad figured the floodgate was open, because after that day he began to spend less and less time at home.

He was working nights, and the only time he really got to see Mom and me was late at night. My mother spent hours learning how to sterilize bottles and tend to an infant, and she loved it. Her days and most of her nights were consumed by me, even though I had a baby nurse. She'd see my father late at night or perhaps early in the morning, and sometimes she even joined him for a party or dinner. Each night, he would tiptoe into the nursery after he came home from the club to look at me. My baby nurse was of German descent and she slept in the same room with me. She hated Pop's nightly visits, which she regarded as nothing more than trespassing! She just about insisted that my parents make an appointment to see me and wouldn't allow anyone to pick me up while I was sleeping. She was well trained and one of the best around. Pop called her "The Nazi." Thankfully, her stay with us was brief.

When my first birthday came, my father was in London giving a command performance for the queen. It was quite an honor, of course. Dad had wanted Mom to go with him, but she thought she should stay at home with me since it was my birthday. He told her I was only a baby and I'd never know the difference. Besides, he said, I'd have other birthdays. Mom, though, thought it would make a difference. And so she stayed. Dad called after the show, bubbling over at its success. Mom was very happy for him. She asked him to sing "Happy Birthday" to me. He didn't want to, but finally, after much coaxing from Mom, he did.

My father did manage to make my next birthday, in 1963, which was celebrated in Las Vegas where Pop was doing a show. I sat on the floor next to my parents, digging my hands into a wickedly fudgey and dangerously large chocolate cake, my faithful yellow cotton blanket with the yellow trim at my side. That blanket went everywhere with me and was the only sure way to get me to sleep. I'd wrap my index finger around my nose while holding the satin edge of the blanket and I was gone in no time.

Being the daughter of Sammy Davis Jr. meant that my every move was scrutinized by people I didn't know and I'd never meet. Photographers dripped from trees to catch a glimpse of me in my carriage as I took in a little air in the yard. The nurse couldn't exactly take me for walks because we lived in a very hilly area that had no sidewalks. Besides, being on the street would have made me an even more vulnerable target for paparazzi.

When Mom took me to Sweden six months after my birth, you would have thought we were Jacqueline Kennedy and John-John. I managed to grab headlines simply by crying during the entire flight from Los Angeles to Copenhagen, and from Copenhagen to Stockholm.

My poor mother. The passengers must have felt like killing her, but there was nothing she could do—I wouldn't shut up. I didn't quiet down until we got to my grandparents' house, and then I slept for 48 hours. The Swedish press wanted to stop by to take pictures, but my mother kept telling them I hadn't awakened yet. So the papers ran stories that said, "Tracey Davis still asleep!"

It wasn't long before Mom took me out on the road with Dad. After all, it was really the only way we could be together as a family. Because I was so young, I had little appreciation for my first tour of the United States. It was on the road that I had my very first haircut, in Las Vegas, by none other than Marlene Dietrich.

For a little kid, Las Vegas is like being inside a giant pinball machine. I thought it was real neat that grown-ups got to play with all those giant toys with flashing lights and pinging sounds. Mom kept me up one night so we could go backstage and see Pop before his show. We were sitting in his room, which was filled with bowls of cigarettes, champagne, fresh fruit, candy, cheeses, caviar and other goodies the casino lavished on a big star. I was happily munching sweet strawberries from a huge basket someone had sent to Dad when the door opened and a ravishing blond woman walked in. I had no idea who she was, but Mom and Dad were very happy to see her. When she spoke, her voice was smoky and foreign. It was Marlene, who had left film to pursue a cabaret act. She was appearing at the same casino as Dad and, as was the custom, supper club and lounge performers always paid their respects to headliners. But she also was a friend.

After talking to Pop for a little while, she came over to me and smiled.

"She's beautiful, May. Such long hair in her face!" Dietrich cupped her hand under my chin, while she brushed away a wisp of hair from my forehead. My hair fell in long, straight strands, forming an ebony curtain in front of my eyes. I couldn't see.

"I've got to cut them," Mom fretted. "But the scissors are larger than her little head. I'm so nervous I'll cut her."

"Oh, come on, give me the shears and I'll do it. No problem," Marlene said. With that, she picked up a pair of scissors from Pop's makeup table, draped her willowy hand under my bangs and snipped away. I could see again! It was the last time my bangs were straight for my entire childhood. Mom cut them after that; I always wondered why all parents think they're great hairdressers.

Dad performed a lot in Las Vegas, so we'd often stay six or eight weeks at the casino, living in a four-bedroom suite. We had our own swimming pool and the nanny of all nannies to take care of me.

There followed a succession of baby-sitters after "The Nazi" left, until Mom settled on Lessie Lee Jackson. Not only was she like a mother to my mom and a grandmother to me and later my brothers, but she also cooked up a storm. I'll never forget her food.

One of the best times I ever had with my Dad was the morning Lessie Lee made breakfast for just the two of us and we got to eat alone. It's my fondest memory of life with father. It's also the first time I ever drank Coca-Cola. It was 1967. I was six years old.

We lived at that time in a grand house in Benedict Canyon that once had been owned by David O. Selznick. Our house was so large, so meandering, so astoundingly huge. But no house was big enough to escape the all-consuming richness of Lessie Lee's cooking. Aromas had a way of drifting through rooms, climbing stairs, penetrating ceilings and wafting through floors. That particular morning in 1967, I smelled pungent onions and savory pork chops, and I knew they were being smothered in Lessie Lee's secret, magnificent artery-clogging gravy. I was roused from my bed by the piquant bouquet and followed my nose down to the breakfast room, where I found Pop still dressed in his tuxedo from work the night before, his bow tie rakishly undone around his neck. He was sitting at the table, surrounded by a mountain of newspapers, with the television blaring the *Today* show. That's how Pop always began his day: He'd read every paper he could get his hands on—from the *New York Times* to the *Los Angeles Times* to the *Paris Trib* to the *Washington Post*—and listen to TV news and have a parade of cigarettes.

He smiled at me as I walked in, rubbing my eyes and licking my lips. I gazed at the mouth-watering mound of rice, pork chops, onions and gravy and announced to Lessie Lee, "I'll have that, too." Pop was drinking a Coke, and I wanted one as well. He told Lessie Lee to give me one. She raised an eyebrow, knowing how much my mother disliked us kids to have soft drinks, but since Mom was still asleep, Lessie Lee obliged Dad.

Pop and I ate in silence, a silence that mirrored the early morning peacefulness of the house. We smiled at each other through savory bites, pale sunlight filtering through the large windows and throwing platinum stripes across the floor. I remember swinging my legs back and forth and hitting my heels on the chair. This was cool. Breakfast with my Pop. It was a father-daughter moment that never would be recaptured. But in years to come, whenever I doubted my father's love, I thought back to that morning, to the smothered pork chops and the shared smiles, and knew the answer. Still, it's sad in a way that one of the only memories I have of being with my father as a child is that we actually had breakfast together. I had breakfast with Mom just about every day, but I only recall that one time with Pop.

Lessie Lee carved a place in our family and stayed on with Dad after my parents divorced. Whenever I went over to my father's house, I'd spend time in the kitchen with her. She was the only other person besides me whom

Pop allowed into his cooking studio on the other side of the house. Dad took up cooking as therapy when liver problems caused him to give up alcohol in 1985. As he did everything else, Pop approached cooking on a grand scale.

He never studied formally; instead, he bought every cookbook he could find and built his special kitchen. It had a huge, round table that could seat ten people, a few color television sets and two bedrooms. It was like a little apartment, but mainly it was my father's sanctuary.

Dad bought an entire mobile kitchen to take on the road. He had his own stainless-steel pots and pans, spices, ingredients and gas grill just in case he felt the need for a little sausage and peppers or some chicken fricassee. Sometimes after a show, he'd whip up some chili—my father's was the best in the world. But when he was really keyed up after a performance or when he just wanted to be alone, he'd go to his kitchen and lock the door. Sometimes, my husband Guy and I would sit with him while he cooked and watch the football game together, never really talking. Then we'd eat the most fantastic meals.

I have few real memories of my early life. I don't recall with any clarity ever sitting with my father and cuddling like little girls always do with their dads on TV sitcoms. Nor do I remember Dad carrying me around showing me off to his friends. I do remember every now and then being in my father's den when he had meetings with record company executives or his agents. I'd climb up on his leather sofa, dragging my yellow blanket behind me, squeeze into a corner by his side and just listen to the talk about singing and songs and records and grosses and money, money, money. Pop was making a lot of singles in the early 1960s, like "What Kind of Fool Am I," "Me and My Shadow," a duet he did with Frank Sinatra, and "As Long As She Needs Me," a song from the musical *Oliver*. It was a tune he especially loved.

But what I remember most of all is how much I hated cigarettes.

I learned early in life that nicotine was the enemy. By the age of two, I was stalking the wild weed like a midget mercenary, snatching as many of my parents' cigarettes as I could grasp in my baby hand.

I didn't know at that time, of course, that cigarettes cause cancer, but I knew with great certainty that they made Dad stink. Mom smoked about as much as Dad, who could put away four to six packs a day. One day, while exiting the driveway, she had taken her eyes off the road to push in the lighter and almost hit another car. Mom, who had learned how to smoke for the movie *The Blue Angel* when she was around 20 years old, quit cold turkey that day.

I was good at my job, and Dad made it all too easy for me because he kept cigarettes within easy reach no matter what room he was in. There were crystal bowls of German glass, sterling silver trays and tables laden with pretty little boxes and Dunhill cigarette cases. Deceptive beauty. I was not to be fooled as I scampered over furniture to corner my quarry. I would break as many cigarettes as I could and leave them a mangled mess.

It took Pop a while to figure out he was being ripped off. It took him even longer to figure out who the culprit was. I think he accused Lessie Lee and my mom. Then, one day, I got busted.

"Tracey, what are you doing with those cigarettes?" Pop asked, as sternly as he dared with a two-year-old. He had happened upon me fast at work.

I blinked twice, the way kids do when nailed, and uttered just one word while crinkling my nose: "Stink."

Pop picked me up and I pushed him away.

"Stink."

I hated the way cigarettes made my father smell. They clashed with his Aramis cologne and made being near him like inhaling the contents of an ashtray.

Pop laughed and laughed and told my mother about my rehabilitation efforts, which made her laugh as well. But I think he got the point in a way, because after that day, he tried not to smoke very much in front of me.

It seems I often added levity to my parents' lives at that magical age of two. It was then I made my first joke, one my father told over and over again to all his pals: I put my two index fingers and thumbs together, forming a little pyramid and said, "milk/pilk." Who knew what it meant? It was utter nonsense, but apparently I delivered it in a way that rendered the rhyming game funny. I didn't know I was making a joke, but my timing was right and I made my Dad laugh.

My only other early memories of family life are my remembrances of my brother Mark's arrival. I was a little over a year and a half when Mom and Dad adopted him. Mark was two. My parents could have had more biological children if they had wanted to, but they considered themselves part of a beautiful mission: Sammy Davis Jr. and May Britt would make a home for racially mixed children, for kids who otherwise might not be cared for or have loving homes and parents. Pop always said, "I think it's inexcusable if somebody can afford it and they don't take a child into their lives."

One day Mom told me I was going to have a new brother, a boy who was special because she and Dad had picked him out to be a part of our family. She told me she hoped I would grow to love him as much as they did when they first saw him. We were still living in the Hollywood Hills then, and I remember standing at the door holding my blanket in one hand and Mom's hand in the other. There before me was a little boy who looked just like me! The agency had brought him over so we could play together before he came to live with us. I was delighted to have a playmate, and Mark and I quickly discovered what we liked doing best: jumping up and down on the bed like it was a trampoline. When we were a little older, we'd delight in jumping from one bed to the other whenever we stayed in hotels.

Pop was on the road when Mark moved in, so it was up to Mom and me to help him make the adjustment. It took no time at all for Mark to become a part of our home. It was as if he'd always been there, and Mark and I behaved as if we'd always been brother and sister. We played together outside on the swing set and in the sandbox where, Mark likes to remind me, I once tried to bash in his head. It seems we were playing with some toy trucks. Pop was with us in the yard—he had just finished shooting *Robin and the Seven Hoods*, with Frank, Dean Martin and Bing Crosby. There was one silver fire engine and apparently both of us wanted it. We both grabbed it and tugged from either end, and I managed to secure it. Then, for reasons known only to a two-year-old, I cracked Mark in the head with the fire engine. He cried and I just stared at him. Pop, though, was furious. He told Mark he could hit me back. But Mark didn't...until he was 15.

About a year after his arrival, Mark got his maiden voyage in life on the road: We moved to New York because Dad was appearing on Broadway in *Golden Boy*, a musical adaptation of the boxing drama written by Clifford Odets. Because Pop was such a huge star by then, Odets got together with the composer Charles Strouse and rewrote his play as a vehicle for Dad. Instead of the story of an Italian-American violinist who defies his father and becomes a boxer, Odets wrote a story about a black boxer who falls in love with the white mistress of his fight promoter. Odets died before he could finish the play, so William Gibson, who had written *The Miracle Worker*, took over. Largely because of my father, the play went on to run 17 months and received four Tony nominations, including one for Pop. But both the play and my father lost the coveted award to *Fiddler on the Roof* and Zero Mostel.

A starring role in a major Broadway musical wasn't enough for my father, though. He was also doing a weekly variety show for NBC at the same time. His first guests were Elizabeth Taylor and Richard Burton. Judy Garland also appeared. "The Sammy Davis Jr. Show" was the first variety program to have a black performer as host since

Nat "King" Cole in the 1950s. Dad's show was canceled after only three months. The National Association for the Advancement of Colored People staged a protest outside NBC, charging racism. Pop said that wasn't the case—the show was dropped because he was scattered and worn out from giving eight performances a week on Broadway and then trying to tape TV specials. But probably none of that really mattered anyway, because the show was doomed from the start: NBC scheduled it against two of the most popular comedies of the time on CBS: "Hogan's Heroes" and "Gomer Pyle."

Pop was so driven, so obsessed with his career that he also found time to start work on a movie, *A Man Called Adam*. He played a jazz musician who accidentally kills his wife and child.

It would be easy to dismiss Dad as merely a workaholic. But he was more than that. He was driven his entire life by a raging sense of urgency. Dad had fought his way to stardom, banging on doors, knocking heads and forcing people to respect him, to give him the same due as white performers. He couldn't just be good; he had to be great. He couldn't just fulfill a contract; he had to give 300 percent. And each success just made him crave more.

He worked like a crazy man to become bigger and bigger, and never once did he forget where he came from or who helped him get there. In what has got to be one of the most bizarre contracts ever, Pop insisted on dividing his salary three ways with his father and Will Mastin, although they no longer performed with him as the famed Will Mastin Trio. Even Dad's *Golden Boy* pay was split with Granddad and Will. But that was Sammy Davis Jr.

He remembered how his father and Will had sheltered him as a child and helped shape him into the show biz phenomenon he became. My grandfather took Dad on the road with him and Will when Pop was about a year and a half. He made his stage debut when he was three by sitting on the lap of a pretty woman making faces while she sang. He was a hit—and a natural. Slowly, more of Dad's antics were incorporated into the vaudeville act, and Granddad and Will taught Pop some tap steps. But they didn't have to teach him too much, because he was a quick study and soon added his own spin. Pop also learned from Bill "Bojangles" Robinson, the legendary dancer who did steps Dad later imitated. Dad's dancing was so good and so mature, he was billed as a midget. Of course, that also was a way to get around the child welfare authorities who did not want a baby on the vaudeville circuit.

I think part of what drove Dad was fear, fear that he would die penniless and alone, like the character in the song "Mr. Bojangles" (which was not in any way about Bill Robinson). Dad couldn't stand the thought, and I guess that's why he often closed his act with that song. He also was the type of person who couldn't say no to a cause. He was constantly available for all charities—Pop was the biggest contributor to the United Negro College Fund. And he always told me he preferred doing the small things because the people who really needed him were the people who could least afford him.

One Christmas, he read about a black family in a little Southern town who had been wiped out by a fire or some other catastrophe. Dad sent them a check so the kids would have a little something for Christmas. And I remember when he and Frank Sinatra did a benefit concert during the Atlanta child murders. They raised over $100,000. He was an extremely generous man and, by all accounts, had been practically from birth. He always thought it came from knowing the hard times and recognizing that people he never knew always helped him out. It was his way of giving back a little to those who needed it as he once did.

Dad was so focused on making it and staying on top that he had no idea about half the things that were going on in his life. By the time he was able to look up, everything he had truly loved—besides entertainment—had changed or was harmed in some way. I know I was.

But nothing could slow him in his fevered mission—

not even the loss of his eye. It happened in 1954 when the Will Mastin Trio was just beginning to get a little notice, earning $7,500 a week in Las Vegas. Pop, who had been performing for 26 years by then, crashed his car in the desert while driving to Los Angeles to record his first movie soundtrack for a film called *Six Bridges*.

Dad and a friend of his named Charley were in Dad's new Cadillac convertible when a woman passed and exited the highway. She started to back up to return to the road. Instead, she straddled both lanes. Dad tried to go around her, but there was a sudden rush of incoming traffic and the woman moved her car into his path. He crashed into her and his car rolled. Charley was thrown from the car and Dad got out to check on him. But Charley was all right and looked at my father in horror. Dad touched his cheek. There was his eye, dangling by a thread. He lost his left eye to the accident. It had struck the pointed cone in the center of the Cadillac's steering wheel.

Once he had healed and adjusted to wearing an eye patch, he went back to work. His doctors told him that eventually he could wear an artificial eye. Meanwhile, his vision kept going in and out as his right eye adjusted to the loss of the left. Pop was putting a strain on it with his thunderous pace. His doctors told him to stop working. But Mom said he was so driven, he kept doing his show. It was like he was possessed.

That's the way he was in New York with *Golden Boy*: possessed. He was a lot like the character he played—a black man with a white woman who never notices the color of her skin or his own, a fighter who commands your attention. And he did.

Sammy Davis Jr. and his family were the toast of the town. People on the street stared at us and constantly ran over to Dad for his autograph. I clung to my mother's leg as much as possible and hated being seen in public. I just couldn't take the stares. From my infantile perspective, I couldn't be expected to realize that not all the looks had to do with celebrity. This was, after all, the sixties, and interracial unions were still frowned upon, even in New York. And here we were—one very dark man, one very white woman and two little café-au-lait-kids. I often felt like a guppy in a fish bowl—you know, the ones that are orange with streaks of black.

My father had become a huge star. Not only was the play giving him added luster, but he also was appearing a few nights at the Copacabana. Mom took us there one night so we could see Pop in action.

Our limo pulled in front of the striped awning of the Copa and the doorman immediately threw himself on the car to open the door. Years later, I'd find out there was a time when the doorman would not have allowed Mark and me to enter because of the color of our skin. But that night, everyone fell all over us—they couldn't do enough—and we were ushered to a prime table right in front of the stage. But Mom refused the spot and asked for something in the rear, just in case. After all, she was taking two small children to a nightclub for the first time in their lives. Who knew what would happen?

People stared at us for a little while; I sucked on my thumb and sat close to my mother. They stopped looking our way when the first line of showgirls came out, leggy and pretty, kicking their legs high in the air. The room was very quiet—even the waiters had retreated for a while. I, too, sat in silence, mesmerized by the dancing and the glittery costumes. Then my little eyes caught something on stage.

"Mommy," I blurted out in a deafening voice. "I can see her underpants!"

Everyone around us laughed and Mom flushed a little pink and smiled. But we managed to sit quietly through the rest of the show. We knew that when Pop came out, we were to be quiet and not try to talk to him.

"Ladies and gentlemen, the Copacabana proudly presents the Will Mastin Trio featuring Sammy Davis Jr.!"

The applause was thunderous. People rose from their seats to cheer him, and we couldn't see Pop. But we heard his voice. When the audience settled down, there was my father, in a tuxedo, tapping his way across the stage. Before his second song, he started to talk to the audience and I heard my name and Mark's, and then a spotlight was thrown on us and everyone turned around...and stared.

Pop knew we couldn't stay up too late, so he thought he'd introduce his family early, in case we had to leave before he was finished. I felt like a guppy again. But another part of me tingled with excitement that my father had called my name from the stage. We stayed to the end of Dad's set and then Mom took us home.

When we got onto the street, a couple walked by and glared at Mom, and then at Mark and me. Why did everyone have to look at me with eyes that drilled a hole into my soul, as if I were a monster with three heads? The stares, the glares, the fawning. I was thankful when I saw the familiar uniform of our driver, and I retreated as much as possible into the inner recesses of the limo.

I reached a point when I really didn't want to go out, especially at night. Needless to say, my reluctance sometimes caused problems. This was especially true one evening when Dad took us to dinner at Ciro's, then one of New York's most glamorous spots. I was about as anxious to go to Ciro's as a tethered lamb in a lion's den. I stomped my little foot, turned red with anger and slid to the floor when my mother tried to prop me up to dress. It was a primo tantrum.

"Tracey, hold still and let me button your dress," my mother said, jerking my little body around to stand at attention. "Why don't you behave, now? We'll have a nice time with your Dad."

"I don't want to go," I cried.

"Of course you do," Mom insisted. I was reminded that a lot of very important people would be there who could write nice things about my father in their newspaper columns, so I had to be on my best behavior. None of that mattered to me. I didn't want to be on exhibit.

Mom finished adjusting a cute little Mary Quant mod dress Dad had brought back from London, and the Davis family was ready to make a statement at New York's hottest show biz restaurant. We piled into the limo, me still a pouting little wretch sucking belligerently on my thumb.

We walked into Ciro's and everyone stared. I spun into tantrum overdrive. Pop was embarrassed, angry, frustrated. He had no idea what to do with a screaming brat. Mom tried to calm me down and get me to behave, but to no avail. Finally, my father picked me up, gamely smiling at all the guests there and settling in at our table. He grabbed my arm with considerably more firmness than I'd ever experienced, slammed me on his knee and spanked me. Then he whispered, "Tracey, be quiet. People are starting to stare. You're making a scene."

I looked around and all eyes were indeed on us. I didn't know why. But I was so mad at my father, of all people, for making me feel like a guppy again that I did the only thing my little mind could conjure up as a fitting punishment: I peed on his lap.

"*Tracey!*" Pop practically dropped me as he stood up, excused himself from the table and retreated in horror to the men's room. Mom took me home. I ruined his night, and I was glad.

Ciro's set a certain pattern for me. All I had to do was be obnoxious and Pop would get rid of me and let me go back to where I really wanted to be. I hated going to places like Ciro's because I knew people would just stare at me and make me feel uncomfortable. I would have been happier if we'd stayed at home in the townhouse we had at 3½ E. 93rd St. and Pop played with us all night.

Mark and I had more fun at home or at the park than we ever did at fancy restaurants or clubs. We were kids. One day Mom told us we were about to have someone else to play with. A few days later, Shirley Rhodes, one of Dad's assistants, arrived home with Mom and a tiny bundle. It was my brother Jeff. Pop was working with someone or another and so wasn't home to greet his new son. This time, my parents adopted a two-month-old baby.

I couldn't have been happier—another person to play with. I was so happy to have two brothers, and I never wished for a sister.

Over the years, my brothers, who had been told at an early age that they were adopted and would always be Davises, gave me a lot of support. We fought like most brothers and sisters, but we also helped each other out. Mark was an incredible athlete, a natural at golf, a great cross-country runner and a good basketball player. He likes to take credit for my basketball talents and claims he taught me everything I know, as only an older brother could. Jeff helped me with my running and was my pacer, my biggest supporter and fan.

My brothers gave me the attention I craved, and I needed a lot of attention from the people I knew and loved. But I withdrew from strangers and new situations, including school.

I didn't want to go to nursery school and I clung to my mother's skirt each day I had to be dropped off. But school had at least one positive effect on me: I stopped sucking my thumb. My mother had tried everything to make me stop: hot pepper on my thumb, threats, bribes. Nothing worked. Then, a few days before school started she told me very casually that it was OK to suck my thumb in school, but that the other kids were going to tease me and call me a baby.

Mark and I went to Dalton, a tony Eastside prep school, and made friends we seldom saw outside of school. My parents enrolled me in a ballet class at the Juilliard School, so I had another opportunity to meet kids and feel awkward and different. I hated ballet.

We seldom saw our father. He did eight performances a week including two matinees. After the show, he'd always go to El Morocco or the Copa or Ciro's or any of the other hot clubs or restaurants and hang out until early morning. Sometimes he'd even do a club performance. He slept until at least 1 p.m., usually later; sometimes he'd fly out of the townhouse without breakfast to meet with a gossip columnist or reporter, or to talk to record executives or movie producers.

When one of Mark's classmates invited us to a birthday party, my brother and I both jumped for joy. Mom had a new dress for me with a matching pocketbook—very grown-up—and black patent leather Mary Jane shoes.

"I don't want to wear a tie," Mark pouted.

"Will we play Pin the Tail on the Donkey?" I asked, a gleam in my eye.

"Maybe," said Mark. "But I'm going to win!"

"I wanna win, I wanna win," I said, taking a sisterly swat at Mark. Mark always knew how to get my goat. He still does.

Pop walked into the room while we were talking about the party and, as usual, had no idea what we were discussing, since family plans remained one of the great enigmas of life as far as he was concerned.

"A party? With your little friends? That's very nice," he said. "Listen, guys, I have a big surprise. Guess what?"

"Tell me, tell me," I giggled.

"You kids are going to be in the studio with me when I record *Golden Boy*. You'll get to see your Pop make history."

Mom just beamed. "Oh, Sammy, how thrilling. Won't that be wonderful, children?"

We had no idea what a recording session was but if it meant spending time with Pop, that was OK. Besides, Mark and I were too psyched about the birthday party to think about yet another outing.

"When is it, honey?" Mom asked.

"Next Saturday," Pop replied.

My mother's sunny attitude abruptly evaporated. "The children have their party that day."

"Well, there'll be other birthdays and other parties," Pop said somewhat dismissively.

Mark and I looked at each other. I started to cry. Mom scooped me into her arms and tried to soothe me. "Your Dad's session is very, very important and won't you be happy to be a part of it?" Was she crazy? I whimpered even more. Mark had an ugly look pasted on his face.

Pop would not hear of us bowing out of his recording session, and Mom never wanted to argue with him in front of us or make him look bad in our eyes. I didn't understand why our being there was so important. At the time, I thought he was mad at us and was punishing us by not allowing my brother and me to go to the party.

We trudged into the studio the following Saturday feeling as if giant weights were tied to our ankles, showing little enthusiasm and a lot of attitude.

Snap. Pop. Blinding lightbulbs. Purring cameras. The stares, the glares. The Sammy Davis Jr. Dog and Pony Show, co-starring His Kids, was in full swing.

My mother always supported my father's decisions regarding us. She allowed him to take the lead and willingly gave her support. Later, as a teenager, I would erupt in terrible verbal fights with Mom regarding Dad, because even after the divorce she continued to take his side when it came to us kids, and never once would she say a bad word against him.

Mom gave up her acting career to be a full-time mother and had looked forward to a somewhat "normal" family life. But our stay in New York was beginning to wear her down. Since my birth, she had been on the road. Now, with three children, she yearned for more stability. She also didn't have many friends in New York. Most of her contacts were made through Dad and connected to show business in one way or another, and none was close enough to confide in. She didn't have that one special woman friend for good heart-to-heart talks. But soon, she found herself unraveling the frustrations of her marriage to Jacqueline Kennedy. After John Kennedy's assassination, the former First Lady moved to a co-op on Fifth Avenue. One day, she invited my mother to lunch.

I vaguely remember that day, because my mother kept saying she didn't know what to wear, and she sailed through at least six outfits before settling on the perfect Chanel suit. When Mom returned, she was glowing. When

I was older, she told me about the luncheon and what Jacqueline Kennedy had said to her: She'd talked about her emotions following her husband's death and shared her thoughts with my mother about how a woman learns to have strength and courage. She told Mom that joining an exercise class had given her reason to get up in the morning when she'd had none.

Mom thought if she went back to California and started us in school, we could begin the right path to a happy, cohesive family. Dad only had a few more weeks left with the show and then he planned to do the London tour of *Golden Boy*. But he, too, thought it was a good idea to find a nice house in Beverly Hills and build the family nest. Dad's staff helped Mom pack us up for the trip west.

Shortly before we left New York, my father took me to the Statue of Liberty. I guess he wanted me to see as much as possible of what made New York so special, because we didn't know when we'd be able to return. A few people noticed who we were when we stood at the base of the statue. I was very used to it by now, and I almost was surprised when someone didn't take my picture. After all, I was Tracey Two Commas: Tracey comma daughter of Sammy Davis Jr. comma. But I still didn't like it.

Once the photographers finished, my father lifted me in his arms and watched me stare at the imposing figure holding a torch high above her head. We climbed the stairs inside the statue and went to the top, where we had a panoramic view of New York Harbor.

Dad joked that he could see Mom from up there. Then his face got real serious, and he knelt down to look me in the eye. "See that, Trace Face? You can see freedom from here," Dad said. "Freedom is a gift and a right and something worth fighting for. Don't you ever forget about freedom. Don't you ever forget you're a Davis. Now, being a Davis doesn't make you better than anyone else. It's just who you are, and you have a responsibility with that name. People might be mean to you sometimes because your skin is a little darker than theirs. But that's their problem. Not yours."

I listened intently, not understanding everything he said but knowing that what my father told me was gravely important. I soaked up his words like a little sponge. One day, they would have serious meaning for me.

Chapter Four

David O. Selznick was lavish in everything he did. Just take another look at *Gone With the Wind* and you'll see what I mean. I'm not sure if his life mirrored his work or his work mirrored his life. After living in his house, I think it was the latter.

Like the famed producer, my father believed the only way to live was large, and when Dad and Mom wanted to find suitable lodgings for the Davis family, the old Selznick house fit the bill. Pop was in New York finishing up *Golden Boy*, and had told Mom to find something wonderful, a manor worthy of royalty. Other than that, he couldn't be bothered with details. When we finally moved into the Summit Drive house in Beverly Hills in 1966, we did so without Dad.

I still remember the first day I saw that grand and wonderful house. It was like being in a fairy tale. The limousine rolled through a set of iron gates onto a large circular driveway and my brothers and I saw our new home for the first time. I felt like Cinderella visiting the Prince's castle for the grand ball. It was huge, stately, magnificent—everything a little girl would want in a fantasy home.

"Is Dad going to meet us here?" I asked my mother. I saw her jaw tighten and her neck straighten, and I knew the answer before she opened her mouth. Oh well. It was always just us.

Our chauffeur opened the door for Mom and we piled

out, holding her hand. My mother stood before the thick mahogany double doors that were anchored in the weathered brick facade and took a deep breath. In her sporty Capri pants, she looked like a young suburban mom. Two eight-wheelers waited nearby carrying the guts from our old house and the new furniture Mom bought to fill all the spaces of our new home—my mother was an excellent decorator. Lessie Lee opened the front door. Mom stepped in first and said in her thick Swedish accent, "I wish Sammy were here."

Mark and I raced through the door and took off in different directions to explore. There was a long, wide hall that ran from the kitchen, past the formal dining room, the card room, the living room and projection room. After we settled into the house, Mom and Dad bought us "Pop Cars." These were huge, battery-operated toy cars you sit on that could travel at fairly high speeds. That hallway became our Indy 500.

Upstairs, adjacent to our bedrooms, we had a large, airy room stocked with all sorts of art supplies. We could do whatever we wanted in that room: paint the walls, paint the floor, paint each other. Mom gave me a little artist's smock with my initials on it.

Mom and Dad's bedroom was at the opposite end of the house, and at the Selznick place, that meant a hike. Believe me, you always made certain you had everything you needed before you walked from one area to another in that house.

My parents paid somewhere between $400,000 and $500,000 for the house back then. The last asking price I know of was $6.5 million. Security was tight in Beverly Hills, but Pop thought we needed a watchdog and got us a Great Dane we called Blacky.

We lived in a great show biz neighborhood. My parents had lots of friends and Mom used to set up play dates with their kids. She'd take me to Nat "King" Cole's house to be with his youngest daughter; sometimes, Natalie would baby-sit.

I can't remember Dad ever going with me on my play dates. He simply wasn't available. If he wasn't performing in Las Vegas or giving concerts elsewhere on the road, then he was busy with television. Pop loved the tube and appeared in many programs over the years, especially variety shows. He was one of the regular hosts of "The Hollywood Palace," a big-budget variety show that everybody thought would be the "Ed Sullivan Show" of Saturday night during the 1960s. I was about three when the show was first telecast and nine when it went off the air. I remember Pop doing the show a lot, along with Fred Astaire, Frank Sinatra, the Rolling Stones, Judy Garland and Milton Berle.

Since my father seldom was home, Mom did just about everything with us, from taking us to school to play dates to parties to trick-or-treating, which in our neighborhood was quite a production. This was, after all, Beverly Hills. Costumes were inventive, to say the least, and quite elaborate, since just about anyone could call over to one of the studios or costume makers and have an outfit custom made for the night. Some people even hired set designers to work up incredible fright scenes.

Lucille Ball had as much fun as the kids on Halloween. She turned her home into a haunted house by draping it in otherworldly black crepe with giant cobwebs and fog created by fans and vats of dry ice. Speakers outside the house piped scary organ music out to the street. And when you rang her bell, she'd answer in a high-pitched, witchlike cackle: "Come in, my pretty. Heh, heh, heh." Never once did Lucy break from character. We knew under that ugly pointed hat lurked the wonderful woman with crimson hair who really didn't have a crooked rubber nose and wart on her chin. Lucy would give us hot chocolate in steaming cups, and we could see eerie puffs of fog shooting up from the bed of dry ice on which they sat. She thought of everything!

One year, I dressed as a witch and Mark went as a pirate. We walked up to Lucy's "haunted house" with my mom, who spoke into the intercom: "It's May and the children." Lucy cackled good and long and invited us in. She and Mom talked while Mark and I ate candy.

Lucille Ball was one of my idols growing up. I loved all of her work and I also loved how she related to her own children. I remember how she had them on one of her TV shows when they were teenagers. I was so jealous: Here was a superstar, like my Dad, who allowed her children to be a part of her work, and was teaching them about what she did. I wanted that for me. Dad always kept us so sheltered, away from his business, and would never think of having us perform on television with him.

Dad never went trick-or-treating with us because he usually was hanging out with Frank and the rest of the Rat Pack. Actually, I don't think Pop ever went trick-or-treating in his entire life, even as a child. How could he? He was always on the road performing, traveling, hanging out with show people in clubs, vaudeville houses and theaters. He simply wasn't around other kids.

There's a great story he once told me about how he walked into a candy store when he was about 10 or 12, and saw a group of boys clutching pieces of cardboard with pictures on them. He walked over and asked what they were and the kids looked at him like he was from Pluto. They were baseball cards. Not only had Dad never seen them before, but he had no idea millions of boys traded them as well. So Pop, who was earning more in a week than most of these kids' fathers made in half a year, flashed a $100 bill and bought a case of bubble gum and cards. The trading started and my father promptly got rid of a Babe Ruth for two totally unknown players. He didn't know who the Sultan of Swat was! But Dad knew every major composer of popular songs from the 1920s on, and the other kids didn't. His head definitely was in another place, and a child's world was not it.

So it was my mother who always took us on our childhood adventures. I remember asking her one year if Dad could go trick-or-treating, too. She said sure. But when Halloween came, he wasn't around.

Mom also took us to Hebrew school at Temple Israel of Hollywood. My father had converted to Judaism back in the

1950s. Pop never had a formal religion—there's no time to go to church when you're in a different city each night. A rabbi visited him while he was recovering from the car crash that cost him an eye, and Dad liked the simple truths the rabbi told him about life, adversity and the courage to go on. Something began stirring inside Dad—he wanted to learn as much as he could about Judaism. So he went to see the rabbi at Congregation Emanu-El and asked for guidance. Pop soon found out that he had a lifetime of study before him. But like everything else my father did, he plunged in and tackled the often difficult and arcane philosophical and religious teachings. Dad embraced Judaism with as much passion as he had embraced his lifeblood—song and dance. Mom, a Lutheran, converted when she married Pop so they could have a religious ceremony. Mark, Jeff and I were raised as Jews. I began going to Hebrew school before I entered the first grade, and I loved it. Those lessons gave me my first glimpse of history, albeit on a very elementary level. History became my favorite subject. It's funny: Two books that have had the most influence on my life, *The Diary of Anne Frank* and Elie Wiesel's *Night*, are about concentration camps. The third most important book I ever read was my father's auto-biography *Yes I Can*. It gave me insight into a man I felt I really didn't know.

If I thought of my father as somewhat of a visitor when we lived in New York, he became a stranger once we moved back to California.

We had been in our new home just a short while when I turned five. Mom planned a full-day celebration. I awoke that morning pumped with expectation. I ran downstairs and found Lessie Lee in the kitchen baking cut-out butter cookies. She also had a platter of chicken waiting to be fried—my favorite. Then I ran into the playroom and saw Mom surrounded by a few dozen helium-filled balloons and crepe paper streamers. She was on the phone talking to my father and I heard her remind him to be home early for my birthday dinner that night.

"Is Dad going to be here?" I asked.

"Of course, my darling," Mom said.

I was happy. We'd all be together and Pop would be home for my birthday. I picked up one of the party favors, the kind you pull and it opens with a pop and little trinkets fall out. Mark and Jeff already had opened a few and Mom was growing impatient with us, but she allowed me to pop one open. The paper sprayed open and out popped a little plastic horse along with a miniature comic book, a tiny compass, a wooden train and some candy. I reached for another while I waited for the other children to come over to play.

The party was a lot of fun, but I could hardly wait until dinner when I would open my presents from Mom and Dad. Dad was due home around 6 o'clock. But six came and went. No Dad.

"Is he coming soon?" I asked, unable to sit still. I was wearing my paper party hat and my little pink dress.

"Your Dad is just a little late. He said he'll be here, Tracey. I guess he just got stuck working," Mom said.

Seven o'clock came. Seven o'clock went. My mother made a few phone calls. By 7:30, she told us to sit for dinner. Mark and Jeff were hungry, so Mom thought we should eat a little and let Dad catch up. But I wanted to wait, and wait I did, a fidgeting filly in pink. I wanted to have my father home for my birthday.

"He forgot," I said sadly.

"No, my darling. Your Dad didn't forget your birthday. He's just busy working. You know he works very, very hard so we can live in this beautiful house and have lots of nice things. Your Dad wants all of us to be happy, and he loves you very much," Mom said, her eyes slightly moist. I didn't believe her. I was too crushed.

I went to bed that night without seeing my father. Mom was still defending him as she tucked me into bed, but I sensed a hardness in her voice, saw the stiffness in her neck, and I knew she was mad. She told me not to be angry with him, but disappointment clung to me as I fell asleep. I didn't cry. Something inside me died that day. Maybe it was innocence, that wonderful quality that allows a child to forgive and forget. Whatever it was, it blanked out, and I went cold. Missing a birthday certainly isn't the worst thing a parent can do, but when you rarely see your father and he makes a promise to be home for your special day and doesn't show, it's pretty hard for a five-year-old to swallow. I decided I would show no emotion. I wouldn't be sad and I wouldn't be angry. I didn't want to give my father the satisfaction of even knowing that I cared.

I didn't see my father until the following afternoon.

"Your mom told me you guys had a great time yesterday. I'm sorry I couldn't make it," he said, handing me an envelope.

I took the envelope, but I didn't open it. Nor could I look at him; I knew he was lying.

A little later, I walked past my father's den and heard my parents talking.

"How could you do this to her, Sammy?" Mom asked. "There's no excuse for not calling."

"May, she's just a little girl. She'll get over it. No big deal. She'll have other birthdays," my father said.

"That's not the point, Sammy," Mom fumed.

"Look, I'm sorry. Time just got away from me," Dad said.

"So where were you?" Mom asked.

"Oh, you know, with Frank and the guys. We started talking, had a few drinks. Some more buddies came over and it turned into a regular party."

"Don't you think your daughter is more important than the Rat Pack, Sammy?" My mother never really raised her voice, but she was working up to it. I had never heard her so angry. And I had never heard my parents fight before.

"May, don't make such a big deal out of it. She's only five. And I said I'm sorry. I apologized to Tracey and I gave her a little something."

I couldn't listen to any more of it. I ran up to my room and locked the door. *How could he?* I thought, as I sank to the floor by the window. Dad would rather party with his friends than with his own daughter. My own father had cashed me in on my birthday! He easily could have said, "I'm going home to be with my kid. She's only five and she'll be asleep by 9 o'clock—then I can meet you guys later." But he couldn't even give me that much and decided not to come home at all.

After that night, I didn't speak to him for three weeks and I didn't shed one tear. That was my punishment. For days I wouldn't even look at him. Even at that young age, I was fast becoming the daughter from hell. I resented the fact that I had a part-time dad. He was always working, and when he wasn't working he was hanging out with his friends. It's not like he was never home with us. It's just that those times were making the endangered list—you could count them on less than one hand. I got used to not seeing my father, and after my fifth birthday I no longer had expectations of doing things with him. I knew he'd never show up, and I couldn't bear the disappointment.

Later that evening, I opened the envelope Dad had given me. It was my birthday present. Money. He couldn't even go out and buy something special for his daughter, or even ask one of his assistants to select a gift. Apparently I wasn't important enough, I thought. And so he reached into his pocket and pulled out a $100 bill. That's what he tipped the dealers in Las Vegas when he won at blackjack. It's what he gave waiters and barmaids. It's what he gave me.

I tucked the money into my jewelry box and forgot about it. It had no meaning for me because my parents signed for or charged everything. One hundred dollars was the same as ten dollars, as far as I was concerned. It wasn't a present I wanted at that time. Today, it never would occur to me to give my children cash for their birthdays. With my older child, Sam, I sometimes give him a little money when we go shopping and then allow him to present the money to the salesperson and wait for the change. It's my way of teaching him the value of money and how to be responsible with spending. That's something we learned from Mom.

As for Pop, he taught me "20 percent." I knew how to tip before I ever learned how to shop in a grocery store. I was probably the only kid at UCLA Elementary School who knew how to tip. That's because many of my classmates had "normal" fathers in "normal" jobs and professions. Sure, some were the sons and daughters of sultans and titled Europeans and other celebrities—like Julie Andrews' daughter and Petula Clark's kid—but this school catered to "civilians," as nonentertainers are called in Hollywood. I envied some of my classmates, the ones whose fathers came home at night. That's one of the reasons I loved hanging out at Robin Reed's house. She was my best friend in grade school. Robin's now a successful casting director and goes by the name of Robi Reed.

As a child, she had everything I didn't have—a father who was always home and a strong sense of her African-American roots and culture. She was my first black friend. Until Robi, I never thought about being black or white or anything. But she made me think about being black because she was so different from me. Her family wasn't rich, they were middle class. When her father came home at night, he'd actually eat dinner with his children, play with them, ask them what they did that day and wait to hear the answer.

One Saturday I went to Robin's home to play. Her family lived in a considerably smaller house (most major movie stars lived in smaller places than we did), not in Beverly Hills. That day, her mother was sitting in the bedroom pulling a steaming-hot iron comb through Robin's sister Donna's hair. It was so strange. I'd never seen anything like it before.

"Oh," I said, somewhat startled. "Does it hurt?"

Her mother laughed. "I'm pressing her hair," she said. "I guess you've never seen anyone do this before since you have 'good hair.' No, it doesn't hurt, as long as you're careful and you don't burn yourself."

I touched Donna's hair. It was spongy and soft and kind of crinkly. It didn't feel like mine or my mother's. Robin and I watched her mother finish straightening Donna's hair, then curl the ends with a curling iron. I felt as if I had entered a whole new world, exposed to a secret society only insiders could comprehend. That's the way it was at Robin's house. Each time I went there, new experiences unfolded. I roller-skated there because the Reeds had a sidewalk in front of their house—something we didn't have. Best of all, there was a McDonald's in their neighborhood.

My visits became adventures in learning—I watched part of my heritage unfold. I ate grits for the first time at Robin's house. I remember looking at the plate and studying the grits as if they were an artifact from another age.

"Haven't you seen grits before?" Mrs. Reed asked me.

"No," I laughed. "Never seen 'em." I'm sure Lessie Lee had made grits for Dad because she usually cooked soul food for him every now and then. But the rest of us wouldn't eat the pig's feet or grease-smothered greens.

I scooped up a small pile of grits on my fork, chewed a bit and swallowed. One thing was certain: I would never get fat on grits. I hated them. I still do. (When I grew older, Pop told me the reason why I didn't like grits was because it was the black in me being overpowered by the Swede!)

Robin's parents had a way of talking, a cadence, a code of sorts that only other African Americans could appreciate. But what I enjoyed at her home more than anything else had nothing to do with race or culture: It was just nice to sit at the breakfast table with Robin, her sisters Donna and Andrea, her little brother Doran and both of her parents. Mr. and Mrs. Reed would do the dishes together. They laughed together and enjoyed each other and their children.

I loved my visits with the Reeds, but I always returned home feeling a little wistful.

⁓

"So, Tracey, what does your father do?"

I was sitting in the school lunchroom sometime in 1967, trying to focus on the latest culinary disaster from the cafeteria. I was so happy to be just like any other six-year-old—laughing with my classmates, complaining about the school food, just blending. Then someone had to dash my dream of being normal by bringing up my famous father.

"Oh, you know. He's a singer," I said quietly.

"Her father is Sammy Davis Jr.," someone announced with great pride, glad to be friends with Tracey Two Commas.

The kid who didn't know who I was perked up, as did a few others who had overheard.

"Neat."

"Wow. Cool."

"Gee, Tracey. You're famous."

"Um, I'm not. My dad is."

I should have felt flattered to be the center of attention, but I wasn't. So I diverted everyone's attention by announcing that we should go outside and play handball or something. Fortunately, my classmates preferred playing to talking about show biz, so everyone ran outside.

By the end of the day, I was more relaxed and began to feel like a normal kid, until my father decided to do the dad thing and pick me up at school.

I left the building with my friends to go home. Just as we walked out the doors, I saw a long, shiny black stretch limousine nosing its way to the entrance, pushing past station wagons, Volkswagens and other ordinary cars picking up ordinary kids. I began to hang back from my friends, my steps becoming slower and slower. My heart pounded a little faster and harder and I thought to myself, *Oh, no. Not Pop. Oh, no. Oh, no.* The car stopped and the driver got out. It was our chauffeur. I wanted to die.

Then, like a scene shot in slow motion, I saw the rear window roll down. It was my Dad. *Oh, no. Please. Get back in. Please don't get out,* I prayed. I couldn't be "normal" if he showed himself, if he flashed his celebrity. Why couldn't he drive himself in an ordinary car? Why did he have to be so Sammy Davis Jr.? I saw the car door slowly open and I began to run for the limo before anyone saw him or me. But it was too late. The door swung open and out hopped Pop in leather jumpsuit and chains. *Oh, no.*

"Wow. It's Sammy Davis Jr.!" I heard someone say. Everyone ran over to the car to talk to him. All the kids thought it was the coolest thing to have Sammy Davis Jr. as a father. Why didn't I think it was cool?

I slithered into the car, trying to avoid as many faces as I could. I hunkered down in a corner while Pop talked to the kids outside. He was Mr. Public Relations.

"Sure, come over anytime. Tracey would love to play with you."

"Sure, I'll sign your notebook."

"Sure, I'll see if you can come over to the set and watch us shoot a scene."

Pop, get back into the damn car.

He finally finished being Mr. Charm and eased back into the car.

"Nice kids, Trace Face," he said.

"Yeah, I guess," I managed. I knew my father had just elevated my status at school by 10 notches. But that's not how I wanted to gain popularity. I wanted to be liked for me, not because I was Tracey Two Commas.

"Tell your buddies to come over to the house sometime," Dad said.

"Yeah, sure, OK," I said.

I wanted to change the subject and talk about the new arithmetic I was learning, because I loved school and I got good grades. "We had a test today," I breezed.

"That's nice, Trace," said Dad, as he leaned forward to talk to the driver about his schedule for the coming week. They talked for a while and then Pop pulled out some production notes and began reading. I stared out the window and watched the parade of star homes whiz by as we headed for our street.

Mom met us at the door when we got home and immediately asked me what I had done in school. Dad went to his den to work, while Mom and I chatted about the day's events.

I hardly noticed that my parents didn't seem to have very much to say to each other. Because my father rarely was home, his silence didn't faze me in the least. Dad was running back and forth between Los Angeles and Las Vegas with his club engagements, fitting in as many benefit appearances and guest spots on television as he could. James Brown liked to call himself "the hardest-working man in show business," but Sammy Davis Jr. made him look like a slacker.

Dad's schedule kept him away during most Christmases and, rather than go on the road, Mom usually decided to have little family celebrations at home. After all, we lived in that big house and a Christmas tree looked quite wonderful inside. Even though we were Jewish, Mom liked to have a tree—a reminder of her own childhood. On Christmas morning, Mom would always call Dad so he could wish us a happy holiday. One year, though, I got so angry that we always had to be the ones to initiate the call that I told Mom to wait and let him call. He didn't. And we didn't speak to our father that Christmas.

My father's absences bothered me less and less after a while. I got used to not seeing him, but a part of me always yearned to get some attention from him, to be able to do things with him. So I was thrilled the day he offered a family outing.

Pop walked into the living room with Murphy Bennett and his other assistant, Shirley Rhodes, who was married to my father's conductor, arranger and best friend, George Rhodes. Shirley came to work for Dad as a secretary because Dad had so much trouble keeping himself organized.

"May, I'm doing Harrah's in Tahoe. Why don't you bring the kids up? They've never been there," he said.

"Really? You really mean it, Sammy?" Mom acted surprised. I didn't understand why. But nothing about my parents' relationship made much sense to me because my mom functioned as both mother and father to us.

"Yes. We can spend some time together," he said.

We left for Lake Tahoe that weekend. We traveled on a commercial flight and Pop followed in a private jet—he never liked us all to be together on the same flight in case it crashed. At that time, I loved to fly. It wasn't until a few years ago that flying began to terrify me. I guess that happens when you become a mother.

We were up over the glorious Sierra Nevada, heading for Tahoe. The mountains were like Belgian waffles piled high with homemade vanilla ice cream that was beginning to melt. Even though my mother hated to fly, a smile danced across her face. She kept saying "wow" and "oh boy."

"It's just like Sweden," she said quietly, as we stood in front of the plane after it had landed and looked around the tiny airstrip at the surrounding pine trees and mountains. Pop arrived about the same time. Three limos pulled up on the tarmac and the drivers scooped up our luggage with an assist from Murphy, who went everywhere with Dad, as did Pop's bodyguard, who never left his side.

"Welcome, Sammy," a man from Harrah's said, as he extended his hand and steered Pop toward one of the waiting limos.

"I'm going ahead with these cats to talk over a few things," Dad said to Mom. "I'll see you at the hotel." With that, my father sped away, while Mom piled into a stretch with my brothers and me. Lessie Lee went in the third to oversee the handling of our luggage.

We kept catching glimpses of the lake as we drove to the casino, but it was the mountains that captured Mom's attention the most. I knew from looking at the peaceful expression on her face that she felt at home.

"We'll go sledding in the hills, children, all right?" she said as we headed to Harrah's. At that time, Harrah's Tahoe was a casino with a little motel across the parking lot for the entertainers. We had several rooms joined together. There was a pool. The casino staff had taken the trouble to stock our rooms with all sorts of snacks and drinks. There also were mountainous baskets of fruit, sinfully delicious chocolate truffles and other sweets, and caviar and patés. If there was anything we wanted, we had only to ask; Harrah's would send out for it.

The next day, we drove out along Highway 50, the main drag in and out of Tahoe, and landed on the California side, where most people stay because it has a greater variety of lodgings than the Nevada side—and that's still true today. There are motels, inns, lots of trailer parks and some really nice campgrounds. We drove through areas so shaded by trees that the sun disappeared. Then we emerged around a bend and into a clearing, the car nosing skyward.

My ears popped and I looked out the window…and down. I gasped. There was a sheer drop of several miles to the valley below. It was like being on a raft bobbing above a sea of trees and rocks. As the car came up yet another rise, we got another view of Lake Tahoe. It was a liquid jewel. I kept my eyes locked on the lake as the road began to dip below the pine tree canopy. Pop had his cameras with him and made the driver stop several times so he could capture the splendor of the Sierra Nevada.

We didn't see very much of Pop after that day. He had the show to do and was sleeping in or playing golf, while we were off doing things with Mom. She took us sledding and riding. I recall that Pop went riding with us only once and that was around 1973 or 1974 when I was 12 or 13. We had driven in a limo out to Will Rogers Park in Los Angeles and rented some horses for a few hours. It was quite a day.

My father had never been on a horse before. If he had ever ridden in a movie, they probably would have shifted him off in time for a stunt double to take over. You'd think he would have been a champion rider because he adored Westerns. He even collected six-shooters from old movies, and spent long hours teaching himself how to fast-draw and spin an iron.

That day at Will Rogers, "Wild Bill" Davis hitched up his jeans, looped his fingers through his belt, twirled his mustache and approached his steed. He was fear-less…until the horse turned its head and they met eyeball to eyeball. Pop froze. He put both hands up and began to back away.

"Come on, Pops, he won't bite," I said.

"You don't understand, Trace, if I get on that thing, I'll be dead before sunset," Pop said, making us all laugh. He walked back to the horse, grabbed the reins and asked a million questions before he got in the saddle.

"This is the slowest one, right?" he asked. My brothers

and I giggled.

"He's gentle, right?" Yeah, sure.

"He knows his way back to the stable?" Uh huh.

"He won't mind someone sitting on his back?"

What? Pop was the size of a jockey. The horse wouldn't even notice him.

Mark, Jeff and I had already mounted and cantered toward the trail. I looked back over my shoulder to make sure Pop was all right and was following us. We were just about to be swallowed by the tree-lined trail when we heard thunderous hooves. "Wild Bill" Davis was riding the wind! Pop tore past us, shouting, "Where are the damn brakes?" He was having a ball.

We went after him into a tangle of trees and found his horse standing alone, nodding, reins dragging at its feet. For a heartbeat, we thought we'd find Dad lying somewhere in a ditch, battered and broken, his prophecy come true.

"I'm here, guys." We followed the voice and there was my father, hanging from the branch of a tree. We howled. Apparently, he couldn't hold on anymore and had just reached up and grabbed the branch as his horse trotted by.

———

That first trip sealed our love affair with Lake Tahoe. We started to spend part of our summers there. I remember driving with Mom from Beverly Hills to Nevada. What a sight we were: A blond, blue-eyed white woman and three little brown children. Strange, if she had been a black woman with three white kids, I think no one would have batted an eye. They would assume she was the nanny. Such is the society in which we live—everyone has to be put into categories—but my mother defied the rule. And so people stared.

Once though, we pulled into a motel in Apple Valley and the clerk kept looking at Mom, really examining her. Then he smiled and said, "You're May Britt, the actress, right?" Mom smiled and nodded. "You're on TV right now. Can I have your autograph, please?" He was so sweet. He waved as we went to our room.

There was hope in the world.

Chapter Five

We came home from school one day in 1968 and Mom immediately told us to sit down, she wanted to talk to us. My stomach fluttered a little bit, anticipating some pretty bad news.

"Your father and I are separating. We won't be living together anymore," she said calmly.

Oh, is that all? I thought to myself. My father was rarely home to begin with, so nothing would truly change. Still, my mind suddenly threw a curve ball and flashed a memory of the morning I had breakfast with him. I began to feel a little sad. Then I remembered my fifth birthday party. The sadness evaporated.

"But why?" said Mark, who was about nine years old at the time.

"Your Dad and I still love each other but in a different way, and since we love each other in a different way, I'm going to live in one house with you guys and your dad's going to stay somewhere else."

"So where will we be living?" I asked, the pragmatist in me taking charge.

"We'll stay here for now," Mom said.

"Where is Dad going to live?"

"He'll stay in a hotel for a little bit. We're going to have to move into a smaller house and he can move back here when we're gone." Mom had really thought it through.

"But when will we see Pop?" asked Mark, who clearly was upset by the split.

"You can see him whenever you want to and call him whenever you want to. You're not going to stop seeing your dad, OK?" Mom was a saint.

"Does Dad love us?" five-year-old Jeff asked quietly.

"Of course he loves you," Mom said, enveloping us in her arms. "He loves all of you very much."

"What about Lessie Lee? Is she going to live with us?" I asked, thinking of peach cobbler and fried chicken.

Ah, Lessie Lee would be the one true loss. She was going to be with us until we moved and then she'd stay with Pop to be his housekeeper and cook. I would definitely miss her.

Our discussion didn't last very long, and when Mom was certain we were all right, I went up to my room. There had to be more to it than what Mom said. Something happened, but what? They never had big fights, or at least I never heard any major explosions. But then our rooms were on the opposite side of the house from my parents' wing, so we'd have no way of knowing what went on between them late at night. I knew a lot of kids at school whose parents had divorced, but they always said their parents had fought a lot. I remember one of my friends saying she had never seen her parents kiss or embrace—they were always at each other's throats. I considered myself lucky that I didn't have to endure the horrors of endless confrontations.

We eventually moved into a smaller house in the neighborhood on Angelo Drive. It was a typical Beverly Hills bungalow—comfortable, but lacking the many splendors of the Selznick estate. Dad was busy making the film version of the musical *Sweet Charity*, with Shirley MacLaine starring as the prostitute with a heart of gold. Still, he managed to find time to buy a dog for Mark, a black poodle named Dinky. Mom wouldn't accept it, though, because it was too much of an added responsibility. Besides, we already had a dog. So Dad kept Dinky, one of his five dogs that remained outside most of the time. I remember watching them outside sadly looking in. Sometimes I felt like I, too, was always on the outside, never feeling like I was really a part of everything.

Mostly, it was business as usual: Mom and the three of us, Pop off working. Separation from his family didn't slow my father down in any way. Not only did he have the movie and his usual road tours and Las Vegas, he also was busy recording and wound up with a hit, "I've Got to Be Me." I hardly realized we were a severed family, yet I suffered a creepy emptiness. My family no longer was whole; I no longer was whole. I secretly yearned for my dad and mom to get back together. It was, I suppose, the typical wish of a seven-year-old.

After my parents separated, I earned enough frequent flyer miles to start a free tour service. If Pop hadn't known how to spend time with us while he was living under the same roof, he became paternally challenged once he and Mom split. The easiest way to see us, he thought, was to work us into his schedule. That meant taking us on the road—even though we lived just five minutes away from one another.

We called him a few times and left messages with Murphy, Shirley or Lessie Lee, and Dad would call us back at some point. Well, he never actually dialed the number himself—that was someone else's job. I always knew when Shirley called and said, "Tracey, it's Shirley," that I'd hear my father's voice shortly thereafter. But there was one time when Shirley called and Pop's voice didn't follow. The purpose of the call was to summon us.

"Tracey? Hi, it's Shirley. Your father would like you, Mark and Jeff to come for dinner next Thursday night. What should I tell him?"

"Sure. I'll tell Mark and Jeff," I said, hanging up the phone. Something new and different—Dad was inviting us over for dinner. We'd gone out to restaurants with him, but he'd never had us over for one of Lessie Lee's home-cooked meals. Truth to tell, that's the only reason I said yes, because Shirley's call made it sound like a "command performance," which got my hackles up. That's what I later called that night: "a happy family royal command performance." Mark and Jeff, though, were very eager to see Dad.

We now lived just down the street from the old Selznick house, but Pop sent the limo for us anyway. It was like the family was still together, in a way, because we were clumped in the same neighborhood.

I looked like a real little girl for Pop's dinner, wearing a short yellow-and-white dress with matching shoes. The occasion seemed strangely formal, and I had dressed accordingly.

The limo pulled into the familiar circular driveway and I felt a little pang, a rueful reminder that we didn't live there anymore, that we no longer were a family. Dad met us at the door, and my brothers and I looked at one another in shock. Dad never opened the door himself. In my entire life, I can only remember a few times my father ever came to the door. One was that evening.

"Who shall I say is calling?" he intoned, doing his best imitation of a butler.

Jeff laughed. Mark shrugged and walked in. But I was not as trusting as my brothers.

My father smiled and ushered us into the dining room. This was indeed a formal night—no casual eating in the family room or breakfast room, or outside by the pool or in the garden or on the terrace. Frankly, it didn't matter where we ate, just as long as we were having Lessie Lee's bounty. And we would; as soon as we entered the house, we were hit by a wall of perfect aromas. Peach cobbler perfumed the air with hints of nutmeg and cinnamon. My nostrils flared with the pungent goodness of her fried chicken. Dad had ordered up all our favorites. We could hardly wait to sit down and feast, until we discovered we weren't alone!

There was a woman already sitting at the table. She stood when we came in, looked at us as if we were going to eat her, and made little skittery, birdlike moves as Pop introduced us.

"Kids, this is Altovise Gore," Pop said, his arm around her waist.

Wow, she must be more than just a friend or someone he works with, I thought as I said hello. She was taller than Dad and very thin, pretty and athletic-looking. Her hair was cut in a feathery Joey Heatherton-type style popular at the time; it looked very good on her.

Altovise didn't say very much to us. She talked about being a dancer and how much she adored our father, and asked us about school. She clearly was trying to be our friend, trying to win us over. But we weren't making it too easy for her. I gave yes and no answers to most of her questions, and Mark just nodded or said, "Yeah." Jeff, though, was a little better and talked gleefully about the games he liked to play.

We were all pretty quiet for a while, and the vastness of the room made the stillness even more pronounced. The dining table held ten chairs, but could comfortably support twice as many. It was closed off from the butler's pantry and the kitchen with a two-way door. I remember so many nights standing on the other side of that door, listening to my parents' friends laugh and talk.

So many dinner parties had filled that room over the years. There was one time when Lessie Lee had made her famous fried chicken, mashed potatoes and chocolate mousse. She had left a huge platter of the chicken on a counter in the butler's pantry. I very carefully peeled the skin from about 20 pieces, devoured the savory crispness and turned over the violated parts so no one would notice the flesh was exposed. My mother served the chicken to her guests and then tore into the kitchen almost immediately. Boy, was I punished that night!

I waded through so many wonderful family memories as I sat in the dining room, and now there was someone else in my mother's chair. This was war. To like this other woman, no matter how nice she was, was to be a traitor to my mother, I felt. Then my father said something that broke through my reverie.

"Trace, Mark, Jeff. I need to talk to you guys in the game room," he said. He turned to Altovise and said, "Excuse us, please."

Why did I have such a sinking feeling in my gut? I just knew he was about to tell us something truly horrible.

He told us.

"You're going to marry her?" I screamed.

I didn't understand. How could he find the time to be with her when he never had time to be with us? To me, it was kid logic. I'm learning that type of reasoning with my own children: For them, it's black and white, right and wrong. That's the beauty of children—there are no shadows.

I felt so empty, so betrayed. Why hadn't Mom told us before we left home? How could she not give us any warning? She didn't seem upset or different in any way before we left for Pop's dinner. He was marrying another woman, but he and Mom weren't even divorced yet! Now there was absolutely no chance for Mom and Dad to get back together. We were no longer a family.

"I'm going to marry her," Pop repeated.

"This is kind of fast, isn't it, Pop?" Mark asked.

"Hold on, guys. She's a nice lady and we care about each other. We're getting married and that's that. I just wanted you to know, and I'd like you kids to be able to be friends with Alto."

"But I thought you still loved Mom," I stammered. "I mean, all of a sudden...Pop, you told Mom you weren't a good husband. I heard you say that. So now you can be a good one? Do I have to call her Mom?"

"Listen, Trace, she's not going to replace your mom. She's going to be more like a friend," Dad said.

"We don't need any more friends," I said snottily.

Dad glared at me, but controlled his temper and didn't get mad. He was trying really hard to be good about his remarriage and was determined that we all feel OK about it.

"Well, where did you meet her?" I asked.

"She danced in the chorus in *Golden Boy*," Dad said. I was too young to even piece that together. Years later, of course, I did.

"Are you going to have more kids?" I asked quietly.

"No. I have you guys and that's all. I've told Altovise that we won't be having children, and she accepts that."

"Thank God," I muttered.

"So is everyone all right with this?" he asked, ignoring my last remark.

Mark and Jeff and I looked at one another.

"I guess," Mark said.

"Sure," said Jeff.

We went back to the dining room for Lessie Lee's wonderful food, but I had lost my appetite.

"Kids," Dad said as he put his napkin in his lap, "let's give a toast to your future stepmother."

I don't remember what happened after that. I don't remember if I toasted Dad and Altovise or what else was said. All I know is that I completely blanked out the minute my father asked me to salute my "stepmother."

During the ride home, the driver couldn't move down that hill fast enough. I felt like smashing the windshield. My brothers and I walked into our new home in various states of unrest. Mom looked at us quizzically.

"So, how was dinner with your dad?" she asked amiably.

I cut to the chase. "Why is Dad marrying that lady? Why didn't you tell us, Mommy?"

My mother turned a sickly gray. "What? Your father is getting married? I didn't know."

She truly didn't know. Only my father would spring something like this on his children without first telling their mother so they would have some sort of moral support.

"Tracey, Mark, Jeff. Come. Sit." Mom was leading us to the sofa. "Now, tell me. Are you guys all right?"

"Yeah, but I don't understand how he can just leave you and us," I said. "How could he love this lady when he loves you, Mom?"

It was simple child logic once again, and my mother smiled and hugged me.

"We'll all be OK, and your dad will be all right. He loves you very much and you must always love him," was all she said before going to her bedroom and calling my father.

That evening was one of the few times I ever heard my parents argue. I didn't hear all of the words, or even most of them. But I knew they were fighting about us and about Altovise. Mom was mad at Dad for not caring how all of this would affect his children. She also was hurt. Despite my young age, I understood how much my parents ached at that very moment.

Mom was granted an uncontested divorce in December 1968. She walked into Santa Monica Superior Court and told a judge that Pop just wasn't into the family thing.

"There was no family life to speak of," she said in her divorce papers. "I asked him many times to stay home more but he never did. The extremely few times he is home, he has not much time for the family."

Dad, always up front with his fans, made a formal announcement onstage in Las Vegas and gave a statement to the press. He said, "Certainly, my not being home a great deal of the time, traveling around the world to fill performing dates had a lot to do with it. But we are hoping to work things out." Dad made sure everyone knew it had been Mom's idea. He didn't want people to think he was leaving her, or that he had been playing around with other women. And with all the publicity his pals were getting with their relationships, it was a difficult public relations job. Peter Lawford was divorced and Frank Sinatra had just separated from Mia Farrow. It was so odd—the core of the Rat Pack all had tottering marriages at the same time. Now they'd have more time for one another.

Pop moved into a smaller house on Summit Drive. It was just up the block from us and directly across the street from Pickfair, the legendary estate that once belonged to Douglas Fairbanks Sr. and Mary Pickford. He had bought the house from Anthony Newley, who with Leslie Bricusse wrote the 1962 musical *Stop the World I Want to Get Off*. Pop had a huge hit with one of the songs from the show, "What Kind of Fool Am I."

Newley included a poltergeist as part of the deal in the sale of his house. The ghost supposedly was a child who died when he was 10 years old. Dad loved to tell everyone about the ghost, and we just thought he was doing one of his tongue-in-cheek routines until a series of unexplainable things began happening.

Dad had rooms for Mark, Jeff and me to stay in when we were with him on holidays. Our rooms were upstairs, just off an area with a pool table and bar. One night, I was in my room and heard someone coming up the back stairs from the kitchen. I walked out but no one was there. Moments later, I heard the footfalls once again; when I came out, the cover of the pool table was off. I went back to my room and fell asleep, later to be awakened by a pool game. I went out to see who was playing and found two cue sticks crossed in front of my door. The balls were scattered over the table but no one was around.

I knew my brothers hadn't been out of their room because I would have seen them. I also knew Dad wasn't playing a joke on me because he wasn't home. I told him about it the next day and he told us all about the ghost. He said it often came to his door, but for some strange reason never entered his room, probably because it was a later addition and not part of the original house. I believed Dad, and I got a giggle out of the whole thing. If anyone in Beverly Hills were to have a resident ghost, it would be Sammy Davis Jr.

When it came to scary stuff, Dad was definitely a prankster—but then, he was a cut-up about most things. One night when Mark, Jeff and I were visiting Dad, he had his projectionist show some scary movies. Even when videos became popular in the 1980s, Pop never rented one; instead, he borrowed the original print of a film from a studio. Pop loved horror movies. They always frightened me, so I was never really a fan. When Dad screened *Halloween*, I cringed while the hockey-mask-clad Michael Myers went on a killing spree. Dad laughed at how easily I was frightened. Then he started talking about old scary movies. He told us about how Jack Palance once played Dracula and ended up sleeping in a coffin in his home.

Pop also talked about Lon Chaney Jr. and the Mummy, and how the undead Mummy would drag his leg behind him while coming after his victims. Dad got this weird look on his face and he really scared me, but that didn't stop him. When I was in the bathroom, Dad walked past the door, dragging his leg. Later, when I went to bed, I locked my door and went to lock the door leading to a bathroom and Mark and Jeff's room, when the door began to creak open. There behind it, dragging his leg, was Pop with the dead look of the Mummy on his face. I almost jumped out of my skin. He got a chuckle out of it, but I didn't sleep that night.

My father gave my mother a generous amount of money each month for child support. Mom also had money of her own, so there was never a struggle. Mom was awarded custody of me, Mark and Jeff. Dad had us on school holidays, Christmas and summer vacations and whenever he wanted us. Meanwhile, my parents remained good friends and Mom made sure she kept Dad informed about everything we did. She also encouraged us to spend as much time as possible with him, since he had so little time for us.

Dad did make a few honest attempts to do kid stuff with us. One morning, the limo picked us up and when we got inside, Pop told us we were going to Disneyland. We were met by the public relations staff—no standing in line or buying tickets for Sammy's Kids! We piled into a few golf carts with security and Disneyland representatives, and sped through back ways to avoid the public. At every ride we jumped to the front of the line. When we got to the Matterhorn, the most popular ride in Disneyland at the time, the line snaked around the mountain. Some people had been waiting for an hour. We didn't even blink as the Disneyland reps escorted us through the gate and to the ride. Pop was with us every step of the way. My brothers and I were just about to enter the Haunted Mansion when a man, a woman and a little boy sauntered over to Dad with a piece of paper.

"We're big fans, Sammy," the man said, thrusting the paper and a pen at Dad for his autograph.

Dad just smiled and thanked him, while the Disney publicist tried to gently brush off the fans. "Mr. Davis is here with his children and he'd just like to be alone with them."

"Sure, Sammy, sure," the fan said, the smile gone from his face.

"Hey, it's all right," Dad said, grabbing the paper and signing.

"Thanks, Sammy." The fan was beaming once again.

"Can we go in now?" I said, somewhat miffed that our fun had to be interrupted. "Will you go with us, Pop?"

"Sure," he said.

We tore into the Haunted Mansion, then headed for the Autopia. We all had a ball in those. Mark and I were especially good at it since we'd had so much practice racing through the hallways of the Selznick house in our battery-operated cars. When we left the Autopia, a small crowd gathered around Dad. The flustered publicist was trying his best to get the fans away, but they just kept coming, like locusts. Pop's bodyguard stood by his side and stayed between Dad and the fans.

"Please, it's very nice seeing all of you, but I'm here today with my kids. Please respect that and let us have a little privacy and a little fun by ourselves," Dad pleaded.

Another Disney employee pulled up in one of the golf carts to rescue us and spirited us away to Pirates of the Caribbean. It was even worse there. Somehow word had spread throughout Disneyland that Sammy Davis Jr. was around, because when we arrived a small crowd formed around the golf cart and people started clapping.

Dad smiled and tried to be charming, but the crowds were getting to him and beginning to ruin our day. "Thank you. Please. I'm with my kids."

The Disneyland people were about to have coronaries. Dad turned to them for help, and they squawked over their walkie-talkies to find out what area in the park wasn't overrun with people. While we sat there, another load of tourists came over.

"I'm real sorry, I'm with my kids right now. Some other time, all right?" Pop was beginning to lose it.

The fans walked off, but they already had done a little damage.

"That's it. We're outta here," Dad said. We were back in the limo before we knew it.

"I tried, guys," Dad said as the car drove away. "I really tried. I'm sorry."

We were all very disappointed, but we also knew it wasn't Dad's fault. We were at Disneyland most of the day and managed to have about six rides. It bothered us that we couldn't have our day, but Dad was a superstar, so people wanted to chat with him. It was hard for us, but we were getting used to his public.

In 1970, about a year and a half after my parents' divorce, my father married Altovise Gore at the municipal courthouse in Philadelphia. Pop had been appearing at the Latin Casino in nearby Cherry Hill, N.J. He didn't invite me, Jeff or Mark to the wedding. He didn't tell us he was going to do it. Dad never even told me himself that he had remarried. I'm not sure how I heard about it— it may have been on a newscast. But when I found out, I was livid. Anger was becoming a constant in my relationship with my father.

Chapter Six

Dad always called Lake Tahoe "Shangri-la." In some respects, it was.

There were many compelling reasons why we moved to Lake Tahoe. To begin with, Mom adored the place from the first time she ever saw it. It reminded her of home, of Sweden, with the tall, fragrant pine trees and snowy winters. But more important, Mom always wanted us to be able to see our father as often as possible. She knew Dad would play Harrah's in Tahoe and appear in Reno at least twice a year, so being in Nevada made sense. We'd get to spend time with our father when he was there working, and we'd also get to spend our holidays and vacations with him.

Mark was another reason for the move. When he was younger, he'd had spots on his lungs and doctors said his condition was aggravated by the smog and general bad air in Los Angeles. The air in Tahoe is so pristine you almost don't recognize it, the scent of fresh pine floating on each gentle breeze. At 8,000 feet above sea level and almost no heavy industry to spit fumes or spill chemicals into the environment, Tahoe is a fairly healthy retreat. Even the water is clean. I remember we used to row out on the lake and if we were thirsty, Mom would put a cup in the water and we'd happily drink it. It was that pure.

We had landed in God's playground. With a definite change of seasons, we could enjoy the brief splendor of fall, a strong winter, a perfect spring and best of all, summer with its sunny days and cool nights. If you love the outdoors, Tahoe is paradise: water sports, horseback riding, skiing, hiking, rock climbing, cycling.

Tahoe pulled us as far away as possible from the show biz world of Hollywood. We could walk the streets without being assaulted, and live in a neighborhood with other celebrities. At that time, around 1969 to 1970, Harrah's and the Sahara housed their celebrity talents in our residential area, Skyland. Mom wanted us to grow up as normally as possible and Lake Tahoe was a small town with small-town values. We could live here as Sammy's Kids and no one would bother us because everyone knew everyone else; we could just fade into the woodwork. That appealed to me more than anything else. Finally, a chance to be like any other kid.

Mom liked the safety of the area. She could let us run outside to play and not have to worry. She bought a three-bedroom house across the street from the northern end of the lake. Liza Minnelli owned a house directly across from Mom's place and the late Bill Harrah, who owned Harrah's casino, had a large multilevel home on the same block. Our house was one of the few in the area with a heated swimming pool. Mom also converted a separate garage into a guest cottage and pool house.

The house was anchored in the side of a cliff. Small boulders dotting the land out back offered the perfect playground for the neighborhood kids. My brothers and I climbed the rocks with the other youngsters until someone decided to build a house on the property. My rock-climbing days were over, which was just as well because it never was my sport of choice.

We had been living in Tahoe a short while when Pop arranged for us to go with him to San Diego, where he had a gig. He chartered a luxury bus for the trip. It was like floating over the asphalt highway in a hotel on wheels. We rode the whole way camped out on a cushy sofa, watching movies on a huge color TV monitor. Pop was on the phone a lot, or talking to Murphy Bennett or his conductor, George Rhodes, but we didn't mind in the least. We were happy just being in the bus, eating hamburgers and watching movies.

Dad thought it would be a good idea to take us to the San Diego Zoo. With more than 8,000 animals, 900 different species and all sorts of rare, odd creatures such as the albino koala and a two-headed cornsnake, the San Diego Zoo definitely has an allure.

So off we chugged to Balboa Park. The driver pulled the bus into a special area reserved for VIPs. A zoo representative greeted us outside with that same smarmy smile we found all over the world whenever people saw Dad.

"I'm going to stay inside the bus," Dad announced as my brothers and I hopped down the steps.

"But Pop, you gotta come," I protested.

"You kids go on and have some fun. I'll wait for you here. I'd only distract everyone and you won't get to see anything," Dad said.

We were three droopy little kids as we walked away with Dad's bodyguard and Smiley the Zoo Rep. But we quickly perked up the minute King Tut greeted us. King Tut was a beautiful salmon-crested, 50-year-old cockatoo that squawked as you entered the zoo, sort of the official greeter. Mark said a few words to him and he repeated them. Then I tried: "milk/pilk!" That one always cracked 'em up! But it only confused the bird as much as it had confused my parents when I first uttered the silly rhyme years ago. We moved on. Maybe we'd see a three-headed giraffe.

We didn't, of course, but we did meet Chester the bear. He even waved to us. *Pop would love this stuff*, I thought. Smiley took us to the elephant mesa and showed us the big cats, various primates and some other animals I couldn't identify then and I no longer recall. It was like being in the subtropics—that I do remember, because Mark and I kept giggling about how much Pop would have loved the zoo because of the environment: My dad loved heat.

We got back to the bus and our father, and boarded to a cloud of cigarette smoke. Dad was relaxing, a drink in one hand and a cigarette in another, listening to Dinah Washington belt out "Unforgettable" on the stereo. It was an appropriate song because this was one family outing my father really tried to make work. It was a fun trip and the zoo was great.

Despite the good time we had, it also was nice returning to Tahoe, which held all the things I loved to do: swim, ski and ride horses. But the sport that consumed me, that revealed a serious God-given talent, was basketball. I was always athletic and always interested in sports, as I tried to keep up with my older brother Mark and his friends. After a while, I knew more about basketball, football and baseball than a lot of guys did. When I was in high school, I didn't think I was attractive. But my knowledge of sports gave me something to talk about with boys. I could easily horn in on a conversation and gain instant popularity.

My passion for hoops began in the fourth grade at Zephyr Cove Elementary School in Nevada. In the schoolyard one day, someone tossed a basketball to me. I dribbled, stopped and shot a basket! I couldn't believe it. All the boys were amazed. But I always had been a tomboy and preferred boy games to staying in the house with silly things like Barbie dolls. The principal at Zephyr Cove, Dick Brownfield, started a girls' team around 1969 and I joined.

The day I discovered I liked basketball was a turning point in my young life. More important, I realized I was talented. It was the first time in my life I had tried to do something and succeeded beyond my wildest expectations. I could hardly wait to get home and play with Mark and Jeff, who were both kings of the court. From fourth grade, I began playing on the girls' team and by the time I graduated from high school, I was voted the most valuable player of 1979 in the state of Nevada for girls' basketball.

Pop never saw me play. He was still racing through work, with his TV show "Sammy & Co.," which he taped in New York, Las Vegas and Los Angeles; his records; and occasional movies, like *Little Moon & Jud McGraw*, a Western he made with James Caan when I was about 16. And he never had time when he flitted through Tahoe to appear at Harrah's. His stays usually lasted only a week. Nights were occupied with the demands of his show, and he'd sleep late into the day. When he arose, he'd want to play a little golf at Edgewood. And if any other celebs were in town, they'd always hone in on Dad like radar, so he'd have even less time. But that was Dad—he loved show biz and could eat, sleep and drink it 24 hours a day.

Usually, he'd send a limo for me and my brothers to take us to him at the casino, or Mom would drop us off. Dad and Mom had remained close after the divorce but, despite this friendship, he never stayed near us in one of Harrah's Skyland houses. He said living on the lake gave him the creeps because he didn't like the sound of the water. Other stars stayed there, though. Bill Cosby always lived at Harrah's house across the street from us. There also was Harrah's villa just down the block, a large, beautiful house with its own boat. But Pop chose to stay at the hotel in a lavish suite reserved for headliners.

Back in those days, Harrah's was the only five-star hotel in Lake Tahoe. It had grown from a casino with a small motel and pool into a grand gaming house. Bill Harrah and his wife, Sherry, owned it. Harrah's was strictly family, and the employees took pride in the place. Bill Harrah, who decades before had broken with other casino owners in Las Vegas to take a stand against segregation, drew up a lifelong contract for my father, who remained the highest paid performer at Harrah's until his death. Bill and Dad remained good friends, and Pop wouldn't dream of appearing anywhere else in Tahoe except Harrah's. It was the only place someone like him would perform because if you were a headliner, you were at Harrah's. The only other major casinos at that time were Harvey's, which featured mostly lounge acts, and Del Webb's Sahara, where I saw Elvis Presley.

It was 1972, right around the time Dad's "Candy Man"

blasted from every radio in the country. I always hated that tune because my friends teased me about it being a drug song. Anyway, I went backstage after Presley's show. Pop knew Elvis, and the King had given my father a huge star sapphire ring as a gift. But after seeing him perform, I didn't know what the fuss was all about. Women were screaming and yelling in the aisles and Elvis was sweating, even though he was still fairly lean at the time. He'd wipe off his sweat with a scarf, then throw it into the audience. Yuck! A lot of women ate it up, though. The music and songs were good, but I guess when your father is a top entertainer, you get pretty used to it.

Pop was king at Harrah's, and Mark, Jeff and I had the run of the place. We could order whatever we wanted to eat or drink—when you're a kid, nothing could be better than that, except maybe a free pass to every movie in town. Everyone at Harrah's loved Dad. He made a point of checking out the lounge acts and letting them know that he cared.

It was always an event when my father appeared at Harrah's. There was a definite buzz. The line would wrap around the entire casino for the main showroom. My brothers and I would get a kick out of walking to the front of the line and standing by the thick velvet ropes until the maitre d' noticed us. We especially loved it if Harrah's had hired someone new, someone who didn't know we were Sammy's Kids. Then we'd tell him that we wanted to go backstage, but we wouldn't tell him who we were. We'd snicker when someone would come over to explain to the poor, confused employee that we were the star's children.

You could always feel the electricity when Dad performed. He never held back—that wasn't his style. He pumped every fiber of his being onto that stage. He was always trying to outdo himself, as if he had to prove something. Maybe that's what all those years struggling on the vaudeville circuit had done to him. He knew he had talent, and he also knew he had to work much harder than white artists to make it.

I loved looking at the audience whenever my father performed—such a mixture of adults and children, all relating to a legend. I remember one time at Tahoe, I sat in awe, drinking it all in. For some reason on that particular night, I began to wonder if I had what it took to do what my father did. I didn't know. My parents never encouraged me to go into show business. But I sure did encourage myself. I loved musicals, and loved to act them out in song and dance. Frank Sinatra gave me trunks of old clothes when I was a kid so I could dress up and pretend I was Barbra Streisand or Carol Channing in *Hello, Dolly!* I could play every part and sing every tune. It was around 1967 and I was about six years old, and I would slide down the railing of our summer lake house dressed in the costumes Uncle Frank had given me, my face smothered in Mom's makeup. When I reached the living room, I'd swing into every television commercial I could remember, then do my Streisand imitation. I'd have a grand old time of it, whether I was alone or if my mom and dad happened to catch my act. Those little childhood revues transported me. I imagined a time when I was a famous performer and people would say, *"That's Tracey Davis, the star. Her dad also sings!"*

The lights dimmed in the showroom and snapped me out of my remembrance just as George Rhodes signaled for the downbeat of "With a Song in My Heart." Pop was outstanding. The show kicked, I mean really kicked. It was the cocktail show; Pop had already done a dinner performance. And he knew he had to leave the audience so supercharged they'd have to work off their energy in the gaming room, or come back the following night to see him again. Until a few years ago, there was an early dinner show with a later show serving only drinks. There still are two shows, but the dinner service has since been dropped.

Before Dad closed the show with "Mr. Bojangles," my brothers and I called over the waitress, signed the check for all the Cokes and snacks we had, and left $20 for a tip. We never had to pay for anything, but Pop taught us early in life always to tip. Besides, he thought of Harrah's employees as family.

Afterward, we met Pop backstage. We opened his dressing room door to an amazing assortment of people and noise. There were mountainous platters of sandwiches, cheeses and fruit, and lots to drink. Pop was throwing a party. He had invited everybody connected to his show: all the dancers, stagehands, electricians, the costumer for the dancers, the makeup person and hairstylist, the lighting guys—everybody. It was just like the parties he used to throw when he was on Broadway in the 1950s with *Mr. Wonderful* and later in the '60s with *Golden Boy*. He wasn't doing it because he was dying to party but because he believed very strongly that you should never take anything for granted, always let people know you appreciate what they've done for you.

He once told me there are traditions that need to be preserved, and supporting the little guy is one of them. Always remember who helped get you where you are, who helped you become big and stay there. In the days before MTV, you couldn't just sing and poof! suddenly you've made it.

"You just aren't a star overnight," my father told me years later. "I have nothing against MTV, but it doesn't prepare you. It doesn't prepare you for being onstage because you don't take the time to train and find out what works and what doesn't work."

I thought it was pretty cool that my dad gave a party for all those people. Dad was still energized from the performance as he walked through the room, hugging everybody in turn, including Mark, Jeff and me. Then he got a drink and held forth from behind the bar, his favorite spot during a party. He knew that sooner or later everyone had to stop there, and that many would be back two or three times. So Pop poured drinks and schmoozed while my brothers and I ate. Finally, we began to get a little tired.

"'Night, Pop," I said, as I gave him a peck on the cheek. "We'll see you tomorrow night, right?"

"Yeah. Tell them downstairs to bring my car around for you."

Piece of cake. My brothers and I were quite self-sufficient when it came to hotels, limos, airports and restaurants. After all, we had been schooled from early childhood by the master himself. The limo pulled up within three minutes. Dad was, after all, king at Harrah's. They even named the bar next to the South Shore Room "Sammy's Rail." That's where everybody hung out. When we were 21, we'd all meet our friends at the Rail.

No matter how many times I saw my father perform, I always looked forward to the next one. There were times, though, when I wasn't that enthusiastic. Often, we would celebrate a birthday by gathering a bunch of friends to go to one of Dad's shows. He thought it was great, but I was a nervous wreck because I worried that my friends wouldn't like him or that he'd wear something weird. But while I was all jittery and anxious, my friends were thrilled.

Tahoe served as a beacon for other family friends who stopped to perform or vacation. One such friend was Bill Cosby, one of the nicest men I've ever met. Bill used to open for Dad on the road and vice versa, back in the early 1970s when he was doing the Fat Albert character. Heh, heh, heh! Bill loved Dad and my father loved him. Even when I was an adult, Bill and Pop would hang out together in Las Vegas. I remember one night when they decided to make dinner for me and my husband, Guy, Bill's daughter, Erin, and Ahmad Rashad. We were in Pop's suite at the Desert Inn. Pop cooked the main course: chicken with a vermouth sauce, rice and salad. Bill did dessert: fresh strawberries. Dad kept teasing Bill about dessert.

"You're making strawberries. That's not making dessert, man. All that is is putting berries in a bowl," Pop said. We all cracked up.

Now Bill took exception to Dad's assessment of his culinary skills. After all, he said, the strawberry statement was complicated: You could have the berries with or without sugar, with whipped cream or without. Ahmad kept laughing saying he was way out of his league with Bill and Dad, and they agreed. It was that kind of night—good fun with good friends.

Whenever Bill performed in Tahoe, he'd stay at Bill Harrah's house and invite us across the street for dinner. One night he made a special point of asking what we'd like to eat, and I put in a request for fried chicken, something I hadn't had since Lessie Lee cooked for us. Bill obliged and, needless to say, it was great.

Once when Bill was in town, he stopped by my high school to use the tennis courts. I happened to be running track that day and as I passed, he shouted out: "Lift your knees! Lift your knees! Higher!" I ran by again and Bill stopped his game to give some more pointers: "Get into a rhythm. That's right. Put a little rhythm in that stride." My running improved because of Cos' coaching, and I also was better on the basketball court.

Like Frank Sinatra, Bill Cosby was like an uncle to me.

School was almost out, and we looked forward to spending the summer of 1973 having serious fun at Lake Tahoe. I had developed a particular fondness for horses and planned to spend many hours riding the hidden trails and exploring the forested paths along the Sierra Nevada. Mark, Jeff and I had a lot of friends, and the prospect of two months of swimming and hanging out was glorious. Then Shirley called.

"I don't want to go," I pouted as Mom told us we were going to spend our summer vacation in London with Dad. That's how vacations always began, a call from Shirley giving Mom our itinerary.

"Tracey, you'll have a nice time with your father, and it wouldn't be fair to him if you didn't go," Mom said diplomatically. After all, he loved us, she said. It wouldn't be right.

"But, but," I spluttered, "I don't want to leave my friends. What are we going to do over there anyway?"

Mark and Jeff were more willing to go along with the program.

"Come on, Trace," Mark said. "Don't make any waves. Let's just go. We'll have fun."

"But if we all band together and say no, we won't have to go and we can stay here with our friends," I protested. And lost.

Shirley made all the arrangements. There were no conversations with my father about this trip. Not one word. In fact, we hadn't talked to him in weeks. He was on the road and we just couldn't seem to connect. We'd call, get Shirley or Murphy Bennett, leave a message and wait for Pop to call back. Then he'd have Shirley call back days later and we wouldn't be home.

Even though Dad didn't coordinate our travel himself, he did make sure we traveled first class all the way. Mom always took us to the airport in Reno to see us off. We never had to touch our suitcases and we never had to guess which gate to go to. This was true wherever we went, because we were always escorted to the VIP lounge or immediately put on the aircraft. I was perfectly content to remain in the lounge, sipping Cokes.

"Miss Britt, we've arranged special meals for the children during the flight from New York to London," a Pan Am employee said to my mother while we sat in the lounge. Mom smiled and said thank you. Then we had long goodbyes. I hated to leave her. I began counting the days until my return.

We boarded first class and continued the nonstop Cokes. A stewardess also brought us a platter of fresh fruit and little sandwiches before the plane took off. We were, of course, treated like royalty because we were Sammy's Kids. We also were three little brown children in first class, and we did indeed startle the other passengers as they boarded. Without exception, they passed us and stared. A few smiled, but most just gave us a bewildered look. I wondered how many would have stared if we had been white. I thought back to a passage from my childhood—my trip with Dad to the Statue of Liberty—and remembered what he'd said: *It's their problem, not yours.*

My brothers and I took over the upstairs lounge on the 747, and had fun running back and forth between our seats. But mostly I slept during the flight. By the time we arrived in London I was refreshed, but I still didn't want to be there.

When we landed, a stewardess escorted us off the plane and turned us over to airline security, who in turn handed us to one of Dad's personal bodyguards, a guy named Rice. My father never met us at the airport himself. We didn't have to go through customs or anything, so after collecting our luggage, Rice loaded us into the limousine and took us to the Grosvenor House, where Dad had commandeered an entire floor. My brothers and I were immediately shown to our rooms and we promptly called room service after jumping on the beds, our favorite pastimes when traveling. About an hour later, Shirley knocked on the door and said Pop would like to see us, and we were herded down the hall to his encampment.

"So, did you kids have a good trip?" he asked after giving us all hugs.

"Sure. It was OK," I answered.

"Great. I guess you guys are tired or hungry, so order whatever you want from room service and get some sleep, and I'll see you for the show," Dad said as he prepared to leave for his rehearsal.

I guess a lot of kids would love to be in London with unlimited room service in the Grosvenor House. I would have preferred being in Tahoe at that very moment, on the beach with my buddies. The next day, Altovise took us sightseeing; when that wore off, we did a little shopping. None of that was fun for me, partly because Altovise kept telling me what to do and I resented it. Also, Dad wasn't there to join in.

About the only fun we ever had with Dad was the traditional hall races. No matter where we were, we'd all line up in the hallway and race. Pop would always win. But when my brothers and I got a little older, the odds were shaved considerably.

By evening, when we met Pop for the show, I was ready to go back to Tahoe.

"Did you have a good time today?" he asked.

Mark and Jeff said yes. I gave a determined no.

"Oh. Why not, Trace?" Dad was mystified.

"Because there's nothing to do here. I don't want to be here, anyway," I said. "Besides, Altovise is always trying to tell us what to do. She's not our mother!"

Pop spun around with his hands on his hips and faced me squarely. "No, she is not your mother, but she is my wife and when I'm not there, she is the adult in charge and I expect you to show her some respect."

I started to cry. "Dad, you don't know what she does. She just barks orders. Ask Mark; ask Jeff. I don't like her. I haven't liked her in a long time and I'm not going to fake it," I said, blowing my nose.

"That's fine, but when you're around me, you'll at least be cordial and show her respect. Agreed?"

"Yes. That much I can do," I said.

We went to his show and had dinner together. I poked at my Beef Wellington and said very little. Dad would ask me a question and I'd give him the silent treatment. Or he'd suggest things for us to do in London and I'd immediately say it was dumb, no matter what it was. I was terribly rude. I saw his jaw tighten a few times, so I knew I was getting to him. But he didn't say anything.

We didn't see Dad the next day, but Alto took Jeff and Mark to a museum. I stayed in my room, watched television, ordered room service and called my mother and my friends in Tahoe. I wasn't sure how I was going to get through the next three weeks in London. Then it all sort of took care of itself.

Dad summoned us to his room late one afternoon to meet someone important. To this day, I can't remember the man's name or why he was so esteemed. But he was vital enough for my father to parade his children. Pop introduced us to the guy and we each said hello in turn. Then Dad said, "Why don't you kids go back to your rooms and

I'll see you later tonight." Dad was dismissing us! So I turned on my uppity little heels and cracked, "Dog and pony show is over," and walked out. Pop was furious. Shirley came for me a short while later and made me see my father.

"I've just about had it with you, Tracey," Dad said, his voice raised in anger. "If you don't like it here, if you don't want to be here, then you can go home."

"Fine," I screamed back, "because I hate it here and I want to go home. I want Mom. I want my friends. I want to go."

"Great. Then get on a plane and go. Now," he said.

I started to cry. "Fine. I will. Now." I stormed out of my father's room and shut the door. Once I found myself in the hallway, I was scared. Then I felt strangely powerful. Good. I was going home.

Shirley made the arrangements and I flew home alone. I should have been miserable that I had behaved so badly and had been sent home, but I was thrilled. Besides, I knew Mom wouldn't punish me just because I was having a hard time adjusting.

My bad behavior didn't prevent my father from taking me on other European trips after that one, and I never wanted to go on any of them. I didn't speak any foreign languages, and there was nothing to do but look at old buildings. Plus, I was a TV junkie and there was no television. Worst of all, my father ignored me.

The next time I went to London, we stayed at the Grosvenor House once again, all on the same floor. Mark, Jeff and I had connecting rooms. Pop was separated from us in his own suite.

Dad traveled with a large road family, although only security people hung out on the same floor as he. Whenever he toured, he took along a sound man, a lighting guy, a stage manager, Shirley and Murphy, his conductor (Morty Stevens or Shirley's husband, George Rhodes), a drummer, a trumpet player, a pianist, a bass player, a guitarist, a wardrobe guy and someone to take care of luggage and all odds and ends, plus his bodyguards. If Dad was in his room and not going anywhere, then his number one security person (Brian Dellow, a former Scotland Yard inspector, or Rice) stayed outside in the hallway, next door to Dad or in his room with him, playing Pac-Man. Whenever Dad was on the move his bodyguard would be at his side, and we'd get the backup team. At one point in his career, my father employed a staff of 28, including people who worked in his office in Beverly Hills. As for luggage, my father traveled with 110 pieces, including stage and personal luggage, his stereo, records, VCR, video library, laser disc library, a table model Pac-Man game and, in later years, a portable kitchen complete with spices, cooking utensils and gas grill.

During our second trip to London, there was big excitement because we got to meet James Bond: We walked into Dad's room one day and found him entertaining Roger Moore. Mark, Jeff and I were blown away. Wow, Agent 007! He was very charming and didn't really say more to us than hello, but just seeing him was a thrill.

That same trip, I almost got shipped out again because Pop fell off the stage while performing. The crew had forgotten to put marking tape near the edge so that Dad could see where the stage ended; with the bright lights blinding him, he lost his footing and toppled over. He wasn't hurt, but when he returned to the hotel and told us about it, I cracked up. He didn't appreciate my sense of humor.

The next day, we were evacuated from London because the Irish Republican Army was threatening to bomb the hotel and other places in London. This was sometime in the mid-1970s. Pop sent us to the South of France to stay with a prince and princess whose names I didn't know then and I never bothered to learn. They were complete strangers. I asked Dad why we couldn't just go back home, but he insisted we remain in Europe; it was his time with us. Besides, he said, we'd have fun in France.

Dad's idea of fun and my idea of fun were miles apart. We stayed in a drafty, isolated villa with a bunch of servants, hardly ever seeing the prince and princess, who spent most of their time out with Altovise. There was television, but everything was in French, a language I didn't know. And the servants didn't know what to cook for us, so we were eating things we didn't like. Mark, Jeff and I would have killed for a hamburger. We had a phone but I didn't know how to call out, and we never heard from Dad, who was still in England doing his engagements. After a while, I began to feel abandoned, as did Jeff and Mark.

I guess if we had been older, we might have appreciated the beauty of the countryside and the Mediterranean. But at our ages, there was nothing for us to do but swim, take long walks, sleep and eat. We were bored, angry and frustrated. There was a swing set on the property and one day Mark took a hard push and fell off. The wind was knocked out of him and everyone was scared to death that he was dying. The servants kept asking him in French if he was all right, but Mark was turning blue and couldn't answer. Jeff and I didn't know what to do, nor could we speak French. Finally, the prince lifted him up and Mark gasped in some air. He was fine.

We were in France for three weeks and Dad never came to see us. Fortunately, Lessie Lee was with us and she entertained us with stories. She also endured our endless complaints and was our savior. I don't think it was possible for us to love anyone more than this woman. She was a godsend.

Chapter Seven

From the time I was 11 until I was about 17, we spent the Hanukkah-Christmas holiday in Hawaii with Dad. It was the one vacation with him I always looked forward to.

We stayed on the island of Oahu, on the "gold coast" of Kahala, which hugged the other side of Diamond Head. This neighborhood, where houses sell for a minimum of $3 million, attracts high-profile people who require a lot of privacy and an equal amount of top security. So the Kahala Hilton was just right for Pop. It is a quietly elegant and discreet hotel far from the tourists of Waikiki. Security was tight; it had to be as the Kahala Hilton was the place where Richard Nixon, Queen Elizabeth and other heads of state and monarchs stayed, along with many celebrities.

The hotel sits on a creamy white coral sand beach that is raked daily. There are no waves on that part of the beach—a reef blocks them from coming in—and the warm waters of the Pacific are so shallow you can wade out to the palm-fringed island offshore when the tide is out. The lobby explodes with fresh orchids, and the suites have extremely high ceilings to give the feeling of openness. Some of the rooms face a lagoon where dolphins frolic. There are also beautiful waterfall pools with sparkling koi fish, turtles, penguins and stingrays.

I think Dad loved taking us there because it was the one spot in the world where he could truly relax. Dad would put on a bathing suit and his plush Kahala Hilton bathrobe and sit on the balcony while we played in the pool below. He rarely joined us and would never go to the beach with us, or anywhere near the water. In fact, I think the only time my father ever attempted to swim in the sea was once in Monte Carlo when Jeff had coaxed him into the Mediterranean. He'd made it to his knees before wimping out. He did, however, swim in his pool at home, but only with fins on. In Hawaii, he was content to cast a glance every now and then toward the water and wave to us from his balcony roost.

The first year we went, Dad hooked up with Steve Lawrence and Eydie Gorme, who were vacationing with their sons, Michael and David. That was great because we were about the same ages. Michael, David and my brothers and I united in a formidable mob with Eygie Rhodes, Shirley and George's daughter. After a day or two, we'd already devised elevator races and baffled the other guests by pushing all the buttons and blaming it on some other unruly child. We went on scavenger hunts for the free Neutrogena products the hotel gave away. I practically needed an extra suitcase to get all the loot back home; it would last for months. We also stole towels and ran up the tab at the poolside hamburger shack. We had a ball together.

When we weren't getting into mischief, we had the beach: paddle boats, surfboards, swimming. Pop hired someone in the hotel to watch us, give us surfing lessons and make sure we didn't drown. We were all strong swimmers, but he wasn't taking any chances.

I also met the comedienne Totie Fields in Hawaii. Totie was cool: She was overweight and loud and didn't hold back her feelings. She was totally imperfect but completely comfortable with who and what she was. I was so uncomfortable with who I was at that age, 12 or 13. Totie talked to me a lot and helped me realize that you can be happy without being perfect. She would let me look at her long, perfect nails and gave me beauty tips: "Don't remove all the polish, just color over it with a darker shade; that way, all the coats build up and make your nails stronger." I hung on every word she said. Her husband, Georgie, was very sweet and he adored her. When they sat holding hands on the beach, he wouldn't take his eyes off her. A few years later, I heard that Totie had cancer and had her leg amputated but had kept on performing. That didn't surprise me in the least, because the woman who befriended me in Hawaii was one of the strongest individuals I've ever met in my life. Unfortunately, she died in 1978.

My brothers and I were hotel experts. We also were room service junkies. We had the run of the hotel, ordering cheeseburgers and Cokes at our discretion. Probably the best part of the evening was choosing our breakfast and hanging the card on the door. They had the best orange juice and pineapple, and wonderful banana bread and blueberry muffins. We always ate in our rooms, never with Pop—morning was his down time. We were out of our rooms by sunrise when Dad probably was just coming home from partying. When he ventured out at all, it usually was to play golf at the nearby Waialae Golf Course, a beautiful, private course that hosts the Hawaiian Open. Mark, who had taken up golf when he was 13 years old so he could spend more time with Dad, sometimes would go with him. Dad also liked to have dinner at Maile, a wonderful restaurant in the hotel that specialized in New Orleans cuisine. He would have food sent up to his suite from Maile, even though they generally didn't do room service.

We usually opened presents on Christmas Eve. Sometimes Dad was with us, and then there were times when he'd be off somewhere entertaining and we'd open them alone. Our gifts from Dad were either money or a piece of jewelry that was so heavy, so gaudy, so utterly unwearable that it would scream at you.

When we were older, Mark, Jeff and I could invite friends to go with us to Hawaii, and Dad would pay for everyone. It was one long beach party. Pop was content to read his dozen newspapers and sit on the balcony while we romped on the beach or gobbled everything in sight at the snack shack. I also liked to hang by the pool and read or just take in the sun and add a coppery glow to my skin.

My husband, Guy, and I would later honeymoon at the Kahala Hilton. It is a such a special place for me, a place of happy memories...the fresh scent of the lobby as a breeze blows through, the traditional 4 p.m. tea. The Kahala Hilton was the first hotel that really showed me how privileged celebrity kids were. We could get anything we wanted merely by asking. If the hotel didn't have the item, they'd send for it, all the way to Paris if necessary.

But it also was at the Kahala where I experienced another first. I was walking through the lobby alone, wearing one of those long, floral Hawaiian dresses. A woman approached and asked me what my nationality was. She thought I was a "native" Hawaiian. I said I was Swedish, and she wanted to know what else. I panicked. No one had ever asked me what I was, and I had never really given it much thought. I ran to my room to call my mother. I knew Mom was white and Swedish and Dad was black and from America, but what was I supposed to say? I needed an identity. This was before African American was in vogue. So what do black people say? I wondered. I'm American? Mom quieted me down and talked to me about my lineage and how special it was. So I decided if anyone ever asked me again, my answer would be: "I have one black parent and one white parent. Period."

Dad used to say that to be black was to be special. I guess that should have made me feel good growing up, but it didn't. When it came to race, I was as confused as a baby swan.

Race was never discussed in our house. It's not that it was avoided, it just never came up. When you're a celebrity child, racial heritage takes a back seat to Hollywood roots. My parents always believed that love comes first, and that the color of someone's skin should *never* be a factor. It left me unprepared for a world that judges us not by our human worth or merits but by the color of our skin. What made me strong and able to stand up to that world was the love of my parents and friends—black and white—who simply didn't care what color a person is. Still, I wasn't wired to detect all the subtleties of racism, those little digs, slights and humiliations that so many black people suffer each day, like New York taxis that refuse to pick you up, or waiters who take an hour to stop at your table or shop-keepers who follow you around the store thinking you're going to steal.

I have always felt more comfortable in a room full of black people than I have in a room full of white people. Even though blacks might feel I'm mixed and not truly black, blacks come in so many different hues that I could definitely fit in. In a crowd of whites, though, it's obvious that I'm not one. Someone will always ask. "Boy, you have the most perfect tan. How did you get it? Are you Mexican? What are you anyway?"

There's so much I never understood growing up, so much that zoomed way over my head. I was shielded, pro-tected by my parents' fame and insulated by the people with whom they surrounded themselves. We grew up in Beverly Hills and just about all of our playmates were white; our parents' best friends were every color. No one cared who you were. And when we moved to Tahoe, there had been only one other black family in the area. I remem-ber how out of place I felt when I went with my school basketball team to Las Vegas to play in state tournaments. There would always be a lot of black people there, and to them and probably to most whites at those competitions, I was black. When we were in the locker room, I'd overhear the black kids talking and I had no idea what they were saying. They walked the walk and talked the talk and were so cool and hip. They thought I was from another planet because I didn't understand half the things they said and did. I felt so odd—I wasn't white and I wasn't black. I was different.

In junior high school, I'll never forget Senior Slave Day. The junior high was located behind the high school and connected by several corridors. Each year during homecoming, there would be a week-long celebration leading up to the big game: special assemblies, raffles, all sorts of fun stuff. Then there was Senior Slave Day, during which seniors would be auctioned off to be a slave for the day. I went along with the program, never saying anything or letting anyone know that the idea of slavery was repugnant to me and made me feel very, very uncomfortable. There we sat, a couple of dark faces in a sea of white ones; no one thought that maybe we would hurt from something like this. I don't know about Mark, but I know I sure did hurt inside. It was weird—not so long ago, selling slaves in this country was for real and not a joke. My great-grandfather was a slave. Now, his great-granddaughter sat in an audience laughing at people being sold. Some of my ancestors had died in slavery.

What hurt me most was not telling anyone I was offended. I was too much of a wuss to tell even my own family. I couldn't even discuss it at the dinner table. I guess that's what happens when you grow up in a school without anyone else who shares your background.

Most black kids pick up on racial nuances at an early age because their parents talk to them about it. My father said very little to me about race, outside of what he had told me when I was too young to understand at the Statue of Liberty. It had never dawned on him to have any sort of big discussion. Nor had it occurred to my mother. Mom and I recently had a long talk about my racial heritage and I told her how devoid I felt of any culture. I know nothing about being black and nothing about being Swedish, except from my readings or what I've learned through studying history. I've always been a history nut and I devoured books like gumdrops because they offered me a sweetness I couldn't find anywhere else. I've read everything from *Jane Eyre* to Stephen King's *It*.

When I was younger, Dad didn't really talk to me

about his struggles. Years later, he did and it was painful—for both of us. There were so many stories, so many injustices. Dad told me about the soldier who had doused him with white house paint and called him "nigger" when he was in the Army. Years later, when President Nixon invited Pop to the White House, that same soldier was part of the honor guard at the gate. Pop told me he looked the man in the eye. They recognized each other but didn't speak. The bigot turned beet red. Dad knew that man realized how rich and famous Sammy Davis Jr. had become and that was enough revenge, so he smiled and kept walking.

I always wished Pop had told me those stories when I was younger. But he was never around to tell me much of anything. And I never really spent any time with my grandmother, Elvera, who lived in New York. I'd see Granddad Sam and his wife, Peewee, all the time, but we never talked about serious issues. We all adored Granddad's second wife. She was called Peewee because she was only 4 feet 10 inches tall. Dad loved her because she was shorter than he was. He also loved his sister, Ramona, and I always liked her, too. But she, too, lived in New York and I rarely saw her.

Granddad used to say, "You're the onliest Davis." Dad reinforced that by telling me I was the last of the Davises and I should never forget it. It's one of the most important things I learned from my father (besides 20 percent, of course). He would tell me, "Tracey, you're a Davis. It doesn't mean you're better than anyone else. It just means that you are a Davis and that's worth something—you must always remember it." I think he was trying to give me a sense of myself, and he told me I must be strong.

He told me, "You know, because of what your mom and I did—and we did the right thing—it will be tough for you, but it will be worth it. It's nowhere near impossible for you. If your mother and I ever thought it was impossible for you to have a good life, we never would have had you."

I remembered his words years later when we lived in Tahoe. One day, when I was in the eighth grade, the phone rang; when I answered it, a bunch of kids giggled and screamed, "We don't want niggers in Lake Tahoe." I quickly hung up. My mother asked me what was wrong and I didn't want to tell her. I merely said, "Wrong number, I guess."

There are no words for how I felt. That's the ugliest word in the English language. Call me fat, call me ugly, but don't call me "nigger." That word is either a part of your vocabulary or it isn't. It all depends on your level of ignorance. I couldn't imagine anyone I knew at school using such a word. I always thought that whoever those kids were, they had to be new to the area. I never found out and I never told my father, because I was too embarrassed that it had happened to me.

Life continued normally for me in Lake Tahoe after that incident, until my last year in high school when someone scrawled the same ugly word on my car.

It happened one night after a basketball game. I had showered at the gym and was leaving with my friends. They were parked a little distance away from my Audi and, fortunately for me, they didn't see what I saw through the twilight. There was gooey red stuff smeared over my car to form the word. The blood drained from my face and I began to shake all over. In my rage, the one clear thought I had was that I didn't want anyone to see it. Luckily, I still had a towel thrown over my shoulder from my shower. I started to scrub as hard as I could to remove the offensive word from my car. The more I raked the towel over my car, the sicker I felt. To this day, I have no idea who did it. There were only 300 kids in the school and I'd say about 200 of them I knew from fourth grade to 12th grade. But it made me wonder.

I didn't tell my parents about it until years later. When I think about it now, I desperately needed to talk to my dad about racial issues during those formative years. Who else could I have asked? There was no racial diversity in

Tahoe, so I couldn't seek anyone out with whom I could compare notes.

I know my father was very protective of my being mixed. I never really thought of myself as different until I was 11 or 12, when I realized that I didn't look like any of my friends. In fact, no one really looked like me. All the black people I saw had kinky hair, and mine was totally straight. I was fine with all of that, because while growing up I never really thought about it. I could just be myself; I felt no pressure from society. My dad and mom did, but we never knew about any of it. Sure, when we were out in public, people stared and some turned away. But I always thought it was because we were famous.

I learned much later about the cruelty my parents had endured. America hadn't been ready for its most beloved entertainer to marry a white blond from Sweden.

I look at my son and daughter; with their skin color, most people will think they are white—I am mixed and my husband, Guy, is Italian American. I wonder what will happen to them? Will people tell racist jokes or make racial slurs in front of them, not knowing where they came from? Guy and I are trying to bring up our children to understand and respect all people, and to know that people come in all sizes, shapes and colors.

One day, though, my son shocked me. He was about three at the time. Sam and I were watching television and a dark-skinned black woman was shown. He looked at her and said, "Yuck." I was taken aback. What could he mean? I asked him what he didn't like and he told me: "Her skin is so dark!" I felt mine crawl, and Sam must have sensed something in me because I asked him why he had said that. He didn't have an answer. We don't talk about skin color in our house, or anything else racial, so he had to have picked up that sentiment from preschool. Ah, yes, as the song in *South Pacific* says, you have to be carefully taught....

Sam looked at me with his large, warm eyes. He's a sweet boy with an understanding beyond his years. But this was out of his scope. He knew he was wrong, but he didn't know why. I tried a personal approach.

"Mommy's skin is dark and Grandpa Sammy's skin was even darker," I said lightly.

"You're pretty. But that other lady is full of wrinkles."

We talked for 20 minutes, a long stretch for a small child. By the time we were finished, Sam thought black was beautiful. Now he makes fun of Guy when he gets a sunburn because he doesn't get dark like Sam and Mommy.

Certainly, the racism I've experienced in my life cannot compare to what my father went through or what millions of black Americans have endured. But it has added a toughness to me and given me a sense of pride.

As for Lake Tahoe, it may not really have been Shangri-la, but it was still home and I loved it.

Other places besides Tahoe held a special allure for me while I was growing up, like Hartford, Connecticut.

I loved to go to Connecticut to the annual Sammy Davis Jr. Greater Hartford Open. That's where Dad took us in the summer of 1978. It was a trip we had made before with Pop and one we cherished, because we got to stuff ourselves with hot dogs and zip around the country club in golf carts. Mark loved the game itself, and Dad often allowed Jeff to caddy for him.

Dad had always adored golf. It was one of his favorite activities and, after a few decades of steady playing, he was quite good at it. So in 1973, the PGA—the Professional Golfers' Association—named a tournament after him. My father was the first black person ever to have a tournament named after him. We all beamed with pride that hot August day at the Wethersfield Country Club as Dad launched the pro-am preliminaries to the Sammy Davis Jr. Greater Hartford Open.

Pop was out styling in checkered shirt and two-tone shoes, just as fresh as the first moment he walked out into the 90-degree heat. Everyone else was wilting. Not Pop, the tropical prince. This was his kind of weather. As he played, about four or five golf carts trailed behind him carrying Altovise, a bunch of friends and a gaggle of photographers. Reporters wouldn't let him alone. Pop told them the real importance of the Open was not Sammy Davis Jr., but the fact that having it named after him could inspire more black youngsters to play golf, just as Arthur Ashe had served as a role model and encouraged black kids to play tennis. It was quite a media circus that day, because Bob Hope and Milton Berle also had come out for the tournament. Pop went back just about every year. President Ford went once or twice, too.

Tina Turner gave a show at the Hartford Playhouse one year during the tournament. My brothers and I went to her show, as guests, of course—we never had to buy tickets for anything, not for concerts or most Broadway plays or clubs; and we always had free movie screenings. Tina was fabulous, and we went backstage after her show to pay our respects. We always did that, whether it was Frank, Liza, Cher, Tina, Kenny Loggins or whoever. It was the right thing to do.

Pop was always so pooped during those trips to Hartford. He played all day and he also did some airtime with Pat Summerall because the Open was televised on CBS. So he never really spent much time hanging out at night. During that trip in 1978, though, he did take us shopping. By himself! A first! Dad's bodyguard was close by as we meandered along the Hartford streets gazing into store windows.

I spotted an Instamatic camera in one store and Pop asked me if I wanted it. I didn't have one so I immediately said yes. Dad had dozens of cameras, maybe a few hundred in all. Along with being an avid photographer, he was also a collector. But the camera I saw was to be my very own.

I was thrilled, not only with the camera, but especially because this was a gift my father actually had purchased on his own for me. It wasn't something picked out by an assistant and then shipped to me. It might sound trivial, but I loved doing what I thought was something normal, something other families did all the time. We'd never had that, even before my parents divorced. It might sound crazy, but one thing I would have loved as a child was to spend an hour in a supermarket with my parents rolling the shopping cart up and down those aisles. Weird desire. But normal.

I still have the camera, although it's outdated and on the blink so I no longer use it. More important for me is that wonderful memory locked in my heart of shopping with my father.

Chapter Eight

Sammy Davis Jr.—Mr. Entertainment, Mr. Hip and Happening—was a soap opera junkie! His love affair began in the early 1970s when he found himself hospitalized on a few separate occasions for different maladies.

First, he fell ill with pneumonia while filming an episode of the TV series "The Name of the Game" near Lake Mead in Nevada. He was sent to Sunrise Hospital in Las Vegas, where he had a few weeks to recuperate. There wasn't very much to do during the day except watch daytime television, which back then—before cable—was even worse than it is now. So Pop tuned into the soaps and began absorbing the minidramas of "One Life to Live" and "General Hospital."

A year later, Dad developed liver problems caused by all the alcohol he had consumed and once again was rushed to the hospital with a bloated and misaligned liver. This time around, despite the seriousness of his condition, Pop plugged in even more to the soaps.

By the time chest pains sent him back to Sunrise in the mid-1970s, he was hooked. So great was his passion that when he went home, he'd have an entire day taped: "Ryan's Hope," "All My Children," "One Life to Live" and "General Hospital."

Around 1978, Pop was invited to play a part on "One Life to Live," and he jumped for joy. I was 16 at the time and went to New York during spring break with my father, Jeff and Altovise to tape his episodes.

We stayed on Central Park South at the Essex House.

Pop had a spacious and gorgeous suite. To one side of the living area was a bedroom where he and Alto stayed. There was another bedroom on the other side with a connecting door to a separate room, where Jeff and I stayed. Even though I had to enter through the suite to get to my room, it was like being on my own. Jeff and I were independent enough to handle hotel living—we'd had years of experience by then—and we loved staying up late ordering room service, watching television and generally having a good time. This suited Dad just fine because he didn't have to worry about entertaining us, and the distance between the rooms allowed him to have a little privacy.

Dad was up very early each morning, so I didn't get a chance to see him until he'd returned to the hotel from his day of shooting. Jeff and I just tooled about New York. Dad had left Altovise in charge of us, but we usually were able to shake her by going to a movie she didn't want to see. We also got into as much kid trouble as we could at the hotel; our favorite pastime was throwing grapes out the window at unwary New Yorkers walking along Central Park South. Dad never did find out. If he had, Jeff and I would have been toast.

One afternoon, I left the suite to go downstairs for a magazine. On my way back, I saw Altovise approaching the elevator from the opposite end of the hall. She looked at me, hopped on the elevator and closed the doors before I could get on. I waited for the next one and when I got to our floor and rang the bell, she wouldn't let me into the suite! I stood calling her name, banging on the door and ringing the bell. Nothing. Jeff was out shopping and Dad was on the set with his bodyguard and two assistants; I was on my own with Alto. I had to go to the front desk for a spare key. Alto was there when I entered and I asked why she hadn't let me in. She merely looked at me and said she had no idea I'd been out in the hall.

Things were going badly between Alto and me and I could no longer hold it in as far as Dad was concerned. Later that night, when I saw him, I told him that Altovise had locked me out.

"You've got to be kidding. Are you sure?" he asked.

"Yes. Positive. I kept banging on the door and she wouldn't let me in. She was there. I saw her go into the room. I even used the house phone and called just in case she was in the bathroom—and there's even a telephone in there. She wouldn't answer."

"Oh, it probably was an accident or something." Dad just played it off. But when he was alone with Alto, I heard him screaming at her about it. Pop was very hard on Altovise and demanded a lot from her, probably more than she was able to handle. It was difficult for her. And with people like me there to make sure that everything bad or out of line was magnified, she didn't stand a chance. Besides, I couldn't get very much of Dad's attention, so I certainly wasn't going to let an outsider get it—wife or not!

I once told Alto that she should never make Pop choose between her and me because she wouldn't win. After all, I was the only thing that ever came from him. Yes, he loved my brothers just as much as he loved me, but I was the only thing he ever made. There was a special bond there, a father-daughter bond, an unbreakable link.

On the last day of the shoot, Dad threw his usual party for the cast and crew at the Essex House restaurant. I had a ball! I felt so grown up and cool hanging out with all the actors. Brynne Thayer, who played Jennie on the show, and Judith Light, who played her sister, were especially nice. They sat and talked to Dad for practically the entire evening. He wanted to talk about the part he had played, a guy named Chip who was a pal of the resident bad guy, Marco Dane. My father had such a way of lighting up whenever he talked about show business, whether it was something he was doing or someone else's work. He just seemed to sparkle, and that night he was aglow. I was envious, because I had waited all my life to see the same sparkle in his eye when he talked about our family or doing things with us. It was seldom there.

I enjoyed that trip to New York, and it was over all too soon. Dad and Altovise were going back to Beverly Hills, so he put Jeff and me on a plane to Reno, and we returned to Tahoe for my final few weeks of high school.

Not every teenager could survive living in Tahoe. After all, we didn't have serious shopping malls or discos, arcades, major theaters or concert halls. We were used to driving to Carson City or Reno for fun. What we did have was Heavenly Valley, an aptly named ski slope. In many ways, being on that mountain was the closest thing to heaven. It's an incredible experience: With skis pointed down toward the vast, shimmering mirror that is Lake Tahoe, you get the sense you could reach bottom and then effortlessly skim across the lake. As you maneuver down the slope, the sun reflects the azure sky, bouncing blue grains off the icy top layer of the snow. It's like barreling through dunes filled with glitter. Your heart races as you rush past pine trees, knowing that if you stray from the trail, your future will be wrapped in wood. Your sights are on the brilliant blue sky above and the glistening lake below, which surges toward you like a tidal wave. That's how I got my kicks as a teenager.

The pace was small-town. Lake Tahoe wasn't Beverly Hills and I was glad. I loved living there and considered myself lucky. Best of all, I was Sammy Davis Jr.'s daughter and no one cared. We were just another family. I remember how great my anonymity was on one particular night during a party at the beach club. It wasn't really a ritzy club; but it was on the lake with tables and a bar, Ping-Pong and dynamite music. A kid from school I'd never met before came over and we started to talk. He asked me what kind of work my father did.

"He's a singer. Performs at Harrah's a lot," I said offhandedly.

"Oh, in the lounge, huh?" the guy asked.

"Well, he's a little bigger than that," I teased.

That's how anonymous I could be up there. Even the boys I dated didn't really care that I was Tracey Two Commas. But my first real boyfriend had big problems with who I was, and it had nothing to do with my name.

His name was Mike Harmon. I dated him during my senior year of high school.

Mike was the real thing, or as real as you can get in high school. We loved each other in that teenage, first-love sort of way. Mike adored me and told me I was beautiful, which was something I needed to hear. Dad told me I was pretty, but I never felt sincerity in his voice.

I introduced Mike to Mom and she thought he seemed nice. Dad met him only briefly. I met both of Mike's parents, though. They were very reserved, cordial and distant. His father was the chief of police of South Lake Tahoe, on the California side. I gave them my best manners, my most gracious attitude, and flashed that Davis charm. When I left their house, Mike and I thought I had dazzled them.

A few nights later, I picked him up in my car to go out for a movie and some burgers. When he got in the car I could almost feel the heat pulsing from his body. Mike was very agitated. He didn't say a word and wouldn't look me in the eye.

"Is something wrong, Mike? Are you all right?" I asked as we drove off.

"I can't tell you, Tracey. I can't tell you," he said.

"You can tell me anything. You know that. What is it, Mike? Have you found someone else?"

"No. Oh, God, no. Nothing like that, Tracey." He paused a beat or two, struggling for words. I could tell he was embarrassed, upset, confused. "My parents don't like you."

"They don't like me. What did I do? Was it something I said? I know I wasn't rude to them in any way. I don't understand." I was frustrated, hurt and puzzled.

"They don't like you because you're black," Mike blurted out.

"What? You can't be serious. Your father is the chief of police in a hick town and my dad is one of the world's greatest entertainers, courted by heads of state and royalty, and your bigot of a father has the nerve to hate me because I'm half black? That's a joke, right? How dare he!" A fury stormed through me. I almost drove off the road. I was shocked, I was speechless, I was embarrassed. Then, all of those emotions slowly boiled into raw anger.

I thought of my father and every slight, every hurt he had endured. I remembered the stories he'd told me and they all came crashing back: "When I walked into the barracks, they assigned me a bed in the corner; the white soldiers had moved their cots as far away from mine as possible"; "I stood there, Trace, while this dirty lowlife painted my entire body with white house paint. It stung my skin so. Then they called me 'nigger'"; "I stood outside El Morocco every night and every night I'd be turned away. Finally, Burt and Jane Boyar took me there as their guests. They put us at a table hidden behind a pillar by the kitchen and rushed us through dinner"; "They handed me a bottle and told me it was beer. It was urine." Pop had told me these stories so matter-of-factly, but nothing could erase the exquisite pain and humiliation he had suffered. Now, my patrician Davis jaw was decidedly tight, as I silently fumed against injustice, especially the bigotry that had clawed its way into my family.

The hatred Mike's parents had for me was born of ignorance and fear. But it was so all-consuming and seemingly omnipresent. Mike was white; I was mixed. We were kids going through puppy love and the color of our skin should have been the least of it. My father and mother's marriage inspired that type of hatred as well—hatred for hatred's sake, hatred for no reason. But they stood firm on their convictions. My parents had carved out a little piece of heaven, a calm in the storm, and decided to marry. Who cared if it hadn't worked out—the reasons their union failed had nothing to do with race. The point is, they'd had the courage to try. They'd let love speak first.

I loved Mike, but could I be as strong as my mother and father? Could I, too, allow love to decide my fate? Mom and Dad had a lot more going for them than Mike and I did, starting with the fact that we were teenagers. But more important, both sets of parents adored them. My Swedish grandparents embraced Pop like a son, and Granddad and Peewee could not have been happier with Mom.

There I was in the car with my boyfriend, hearing him tell me about his bigoted parents. I couldn't immediately decide what to do about him. I knew only that I was hurting and I was mad. So I took the path of least resistance and said, "If you don't want to go out with me anymore, I understand."

Mike looked crushed, as though I had slapped him. "No way. I'm not breaking off with you," he said.

"Then what, Mike? What are we talking about? I mean, didn't you stand up to your parents? What did you say to them?" Mike studied the dashboard and wouldn't look at me. We drove up around Heavenly Valley and parked.

"Now, tell me exactly what happened."

He ran his hand through his hair and began. His parents had confronted him and asked why he was seeing me; he said he loved me. His mother slapped him hard in the face! Then his father, Mr. Chief of Police, pushed Mike around and hit him. "I don't want my son marrying a nigger, and the only thing worse than a nigger," he said, "is a white person who would marry one." That's when Mike swung back, and he and his father started fighting for real. By the end of the night, the Harmons told Mike if he continued to date me, they wouldn't support him anymore.

"Trace, I told them I wouldn't give you up," he said.

"So, they cut you off?"

"Yup. The whole nine yards," he said.

Mike's parents had promised to give him a new car if he kept a B average his senior year, which he did. They also said they'd pay for college. Now, because of me, Mike would have to shoulder the cost of his education by himself. I felt so torn. Part of me was happy that a man loved me so much he would stick by his principles and make a sacrifice. Another part was sorry he would suffer.

It was 4 a.m. by the time I dropped Mike at his house. When I got home, my mother was half awake. I entered the house crying and told her what had happened. She was soothing and tried to comfort me; I guess my bout with bigotry reopened the wounds she had sustained when she was with Dad. We held each other. Maybe we both thought of Dad. He was wrong: Lake Tahoe was not Shangri-la after all.

Mike and I continued to date. He took me to the prom on the HMS *Dixie*, a big paddlewheel boat, and came to my graduation from George Whittell High School one cool but sunny spring day. All the parents and other guests were gathered in the gym. Mom was there with Jeff and Mark. Pop was there, too…I thought. All the graduates were in the hallway waiting to march in, but the administrator held us up.

"We're going to start late," he announced.

No one seemed to know what was going on, and everyone was getting uncomfortable in those wretched caps and gowns. I began to get a bad feeling about it all, so I left my place and went over to one of the teachers.

"Well, Tracey, we can't start yet because we're waiting for your father," she said.

I didn't know what to say. I was so embarrassed. "You can start. I mean, he's not a guest speaker or anything like that," I said.

"Oh, no. We couldn't do that, not after everything your Dad has done for the school." And with that she flitted away to check on the band.

I crawled back to the line, beet red. I was the only student who knew the reason why we hadn't started yet. Sammy Davis Jr. would be there and the world had to stop. They loved him at my high school because he had built the baseball field and given money to the library. He also had sung the national anthem at homecoming one year. Now, that was really something, because megastars certainly didn't entertain at high school football games. I mean, it wasn't the Super Bowl.

We stayed restless for another 30 minutes, then the band began warming up and, finally, we marched to our seats. I looked out into the audience and yup, there was Pop, clicking away: He had three cameras with him and was furiously taking pictures with all the other parents. I was almost surprised to see him do such a normal parent thing.

We took my diploma back to Mom's house where she

My grandfather, Dad and Uncle Will Mastin (on the right). Will wasn't a blood uncle, they weren't even related. But Pop said that a tighter family could not have existed.

This picture stuns me. Dad hated the water and the sand and he couldn't swim. It must have been a publicity stunt.

Granddad and Rosa B. Davis , the two people who raised my father. Rosa B. was my father's grandmother and she would live with my parents for a time after their marriage. My mother adored her.

Dad with pal Jerry Lewis. They would remain lifelong friends, working for "Jerry's Kids" and performing together numerous times.

Pop and Marilyn Monroe were great buddies. My mom would also become a friend, and she said there wasn't anyone who didn't love Marilyn.

Dad, Betty Comden and Adolph Green.

When I was little, once my father had sung a song twice, I had it memorized. I couldn't understand why they would sing it over and over again in the studio.

Bernie Abramson

Dad taping one of his television specials. He was such a perfectionist. He used to tell me, "Astaire's a perfectionist. Me, I'm just a hoofer."

Bernie Abramson

Dad on stage with Frank Sinatra and Dean Martin. They were called "The Rat Pack" and he told me these were the best times he ever had. They ruled the day and had a blast doing it.

The Rothman Family Collection

Dad and Elvis Presley. Elvis would later give Dad a gun to add to his collection.

My father hated horses but he loved dressing up in western gear. Here he is on a movie set.

Dad and his best pals clowning backstage. "Sure I'm dying, and Frank's gonna do another ten years just to spite me," Dad told me at Cedars-Sinai. He would go to the ends of the earth for these guys.

I love this picture of my parents. I think it shows how wide open their
spirits were.

My mother and father on the dock at Lake Tahoe. We would later move there after the divorce.

Dad and his best man and best friend, Frank Sinatra, at my parents' wedding in November 1960.

My father and mother walk toward the rabbi at their wedding. My dad looks so serious, but I always thought my mom looked like a princess.

Dad's idea of living large.

Chapter Nine

When it came time to figure out my future, I had absolutely no idea what I wanted to do. At some point in my life, I had considered being a lawyer or doing something in entertainment. But the only career I ever seriously flirted with was acting, and I didn't make a strong effort in that direction. All I really knew was that I loved history, basketball and Mike. So when he decided to go to Santa Rosa College, a two-year school, I followed.

Santa Rosa was about four hours from Tahoe, north of San Francisco. I arrived in the fall of 1979 in my pimpmobile, and moved into the apartment Dad had rented for me and Diane. It was fully equipped: microwave, stereo components, television with cable. I joined the basketball team, studied hard, spent a lot of time with Mike and fell into the routine of college life.

What I didn't fall into, though, was drugs. Drugs turned me off. It's not as if I was a little goody two-shoes—far from it. I'd never snitch or turn in my friends who were smoking marijuana. My resistance to drugs went back to childhood. In 1969, after my parents divorced and we had moved down the street to Angelo Drive, I remember lying in bed one night listening to the radio. A news report came on that Art Linkletter's 20-year-old daughter, Diane, had jumped from a Hollywood apartment building to her death. She had been using LSD. It freaked me out so badly, I had to sleep with my mother that night. It also left a lasting impression on me about drugs.

Another reason I didn't embrace drugs was because of my father's endless chain of cigarettes. Smoking had so turned me off, I couldn't consider polluting my lungs with grass, although I did try it once or twice. My mother never used drugs, but I knew Dad did. It wasn't until I was an adult and he and I became close that I found out the extent of his abuse. While I was growing up, my father never took anything in front of us except alcohol and, of course, nicotine. I once discovered a bag of grass in Altovise's closet and I told Dad about it. He was upset with her for having it while my brothers and I were around.

There were times over the years when I wondered about all of Pop's energy and suspected he might be doing cocaine, as certainly so many entertainers did. It wasn't until I was married that Dad told me all about his drug days.

Guy and I had gone to Las Vegas to see Pop, who was headlining at the Desert Inn. One night, he invited some old vaudeville friends over for dinner. The Augustinos had performed as a balancing act and played the same circuit as the Will Mastin Trio. Mr. Augustino looked like something out of an old Charles Atlas magazine: He was about 5 feet 9 inches and built like the letter V. His shoulders were massive and he was still in great shape. His wife was a petite blonde who could have been a magician's assistant. Their act consisted of his balancing her in various positions. As they rehashed their old stories, you could only imagine what the act had been like. Pop's face lit up hearing about the old times, as it always did whenever talk turned to entertainment. It warmed my heart to see the gleam in his eye and hear the lightness of his voice. The Augustinos didn't perform anymore, and Mr. Augustino had become a stagehand. Whenever Dad performed in Vegas, he always requested that Mr. Augustino be put on his crew. This wasn't an act of charity, it was simply something that anyone in show business at that time would do for someone else in the business.

Guy and I listened to the three of them talk about the old days. Mr. Augustino talked about a time when musicians had gone on strike on the Vegas strip and Pop had refused to cross the picket line. He'd gone home and waited out his gig. No heroics, just my father's respect for live talent. Then Mr. Augustino shook his head, lamenting a time years ago when Dad hadn't been allowed to sleep in the same hotel in which he performed.

"How could you possibly let that happen, Pop? Why didn't you just tell them to shove it?" I said, angered by the injustice.

Mr. Augustino leaned over, took my hand and said, "He didn't have a choice, honey." I knew that, but the sadness in this man's face was incredible. And the warmth between the Augustinos and Pop was real.

Later that night, Guy and I ended up gambling with Pop, but I couldn't stop talking about the Augustinos. I asked Dad what had happened to their career. He explained that when vaudeville died out, so did the demand for many of those acts, which were weeded out by the process of natural selection.

"How unlike today," I said, "when so many acts fold because of drugs or hard living."

"Yeah, drugs get a lot of people," Pop said. "I know I certainly had my fill." Then he laughed as he began to tell Guy and me about his wild days and the coke parties he used to have with other stars.

It was always understood at these affairs that if you came, you'd do drugs—everyone had to participate so no one could snitch. After all, these parties hosted some big names, enough to fill the supermarket tabloids with years of stories. Pop said they coaxed the unwilling just so they wouldn't squeal. He picked up a spoon from the table, pretending it contained coke, and thrust it in our faces. "Oh, you *will* have some of this," he said. We all laughed at Dad's imitation of his debauchery, until he turned serious again.

"One thing about those days really shook me. That was Frank," he said. "Frank stopped talking to me. Didn't want anything to do with me as long as I was doing drugs. I broke his heart by getting involved with coke and he broke mine when he turned his back on me. But it was the best thing a good friend could ever do. Man, did Frank wake me up. I love him for it."

"I feel so weird not knowing about any of this," I said. "I mean, I never saw you do anything, Pop."

"Yeah, well, I wasn't going to do anything in front of you. Tell me, Trace, what drugs have you done? It's all right to admit it, because I'm in no position to be angry."

"Actually, Pop, I only tried pot once or twice. I've never been interested in drugs," I said.

"You're kidding," he said.

"No, honest. Anyway, Pop, you've done enough for both of us, don't you think?" We all laughed.

Then I remembered "the nail."

When I was 15, Dad came up to Tahoe to perform. Mark, Jeff and I went to Harrah's to see him. We immediately zoomed in on Dad's one red fingernail. It was spooky. We asked why he had his nail painted red and he wouldn't answer us. The next day, I went alone to see Dad and I was determined to pin him down about "the nail."

"All right, Pop, what's up with that nail?" I demanded.

He was a little agitated, making quick moves, and he wouldn't sit still. "Well, I guess you're old enough to know," he said.

And I thought, *Oh, God. Now what?* Dad could be so weird sometimes. He lit a cigarette and explained through a curtain of smoke, "It's a symbol of devil worship."

I looked at him as if he had three heads. "What?"

"Yeah, well, I'm studying with these people and it's our symbol," he said as he started to pace around the room.

"What are you talking about, Dad? We're Jews."

"Well, yes. It's just that sometimes when I'm at my lowest and feeling very down, when I don't have any strength or energy, I call on it and it just comes through me and it gives me energy," he said, grinding his teeth while he talked, his face contorting with tension. He scared me; I just wanted to get out of that room and away from him, but he kept talking. He was right up close to me, as if he wanted me to feel what he was feeling, to share whatever insane knowledge he knew.

"I can just feel its strength and energy coming through my body, and I feel so powerful." Then he abruptly stopped talking, as if he were a puppet and someone had pulled a string. He caught himself and backed away from me.

"I don't want to know about any of that, Dad. It's just too weird. I mean, why are you doing it? I don't understand," I said, walking toward the door to leave.

"Don't pay it any mind, Trace," was all he said as I left.

My father stayed in that satanic cult for almost two years. One day he just said no more. He had had enough. It was the same with drugs. Once he'd decided to stop doing coke, he just quit.

I met my future husband through my friend Diane, who was dating his roommate. Guy, a player on the men's basketball team, and I passed each other on the court for five or six weeks before we actually ever spoke. My team would practice first, then go off and the men's team would take over. Guy never really looked at me—I always was a sweaty heap after practice. At a party one night he didn't even recognize me. We spent some time talking and I thought he was nice. My heart still belonged to Mike, but if anyone could ease it away, it was Guy. I really liked him. A short time after that party, I was with Diane at Guy's house. He wanted to watch a movie but didn't have cable. I did, so I took him over to my place.

Mike drove up just as we were going in, and he snapped. "What are you doing?" he demanded, without trying to find out who was who and what was what.

I walked over to Mike to calm him, to reassure him that Guy was just a friend stopping by to watch a movie. I even asked him to stay as well. But he'd have nothing of it and went home. I stayed with Guy and watched the movie, and went to see Mike later that night. We made love and immediately afterward, he leaped out of the bed and screamed at me to get out.

"I just screwed you like you screwed me with Guy, so get out," he yelled.

"What are you talking about? I haven't done anything. I've always been faithful to you," I said. It didn't matter. Mike was convinced that I had cheated and this was his way of getting back at me.

It was an ugly breakup, but from it rose a truer, more mature love. Guy and I started dating. I spent several nights at his house and when I finally left, I closed the front door and said to myself with a warm, knowing glow, "I'm gonna marry him. I know it." Within two months of breaking up with Mike, Guy was practically living with me.

Diane and I were roommates for a while, until I got my own apartment, since Dad was paying for everything. The apartment I wanted had an extremely long waiting list, but I jumped to the top by having Diane pose as my father's secretary, expressing his concern that Sammy Davis Jr.'s daughter live in the best possible building. That did the trick. I moved in a month later with my color TV, cable and stereo system. I often joked with Guy that the only reason he ever fell in love with me was because of HBO. He lived in a party animal house with two other roommates, a lot of noise and not much of anything else.

When Guy graduated from Santa Rosa, he won a basketball scholarship to California State University, Northridge. That meant he would be moving to Los Angeles, while I spent another year at Santa Rosa. I watched him drive away in his '69 Mustang and cried my heart out. I couldn't bear being separated from him. But I also was committed to remaining on the women's team. That I wouldn't give up for anything—or so I thought.

I sent Guy airplane tickets so he could easily make the run between L.A. and San Francisco to see me, but eventually the visits began to taper off. The strain of a long-distance relationship while in college was just too much for him. I knew, just as my mother had known with my father, that I could move to Los Angeles and make a go of it or let the relationship end.

So I dropped out of school and moved to L.A., where I decided I could find a job and live with Guy. Guy panicked. To begin with, he was bunking temporarily with his god-mother in downtown L.A. and didn't have a place for me to stay. More important, he simply wasn't prepared to make that kind of commitment to me, and my move overwhelmed him.

My mother was furious that I had dropped out, and she kept telling me over and over that I'd never go back, that I'd ruined my future. Worst of all was my father: He flipped out. I decided to talk to him face-to-face about my decision and about getting a place to stay. I had always thought Pop's most receptive time was early morning, so that's when I went to his house in Beverly Hills.

I found Pop sitting in the breakfast nook attending to his daily ritual of coffee, newspapers and a blaring TV news show. He was cloaked in cigarette smoke as he puzzled over the events of the day. Pop couldn't have been more relaxed, as he sat in one of his many V-neck sweaters, jeans and black Gucci slippers. That was his favorite outfit and I always loved him for it.

I was a little apprehensive about discussing my decision with Dad. After all, I was the first Davis ever to attend college, and my success was very important to Dad. Pop had never gone to any school in his entire life; he was totally self-educated. He didn't learn how to read until a sergeant taught him in the Army. That's something to really think about: It was unheard of for any black entertainer to reach the pinnacle that Dad had, and to understand the mechanics of the business side and stay on top. My father, a self-taught man, accomplished that. And now, here I was giving up the one thing he would never have. It was my intent, though, to work for the rest of the semester and then go back to school in L.A.—I was not abandoning college, merely taking a semester off.

"You know you're never going to find a job. People are out of work left and right here. I don't know what you're thinking," Dad said, after I had presented my feeble explanation of what I planned to do.

"Pop, I know I can get a job. You're wrong. I have all the papers with me and I'm already making calls," I said.

"Puh! You're never going to find anything. There are a lot of applicants and some of them even have degrees," he said.

"I'll get something, you'll see. All I want from you is a place to stay. Please may I stay here with you and Alto until I find something for myself?" I pleaded.

"No," he said, pouring himself some more coffee.

"What? You won't let me stay here? Pop, you only have about six bedrooms and 10,000 square feet. I won't be in the way and it will only be for a few days until I get a job."

"No. You quit school, you figure it out," he said.

I just sat there sipping a Coke, staring at Dad in disbelief. I hated him. I thought about my brother Mark, who, after high school, had sold the new car Pop had given him, gone through some of his trust fund and dropped out in Hawaii to find himself—without telling anyone. After Dad found out where he was, he'd fly him back to Los Angeles whenever he wanted to see Mark and allow him to live in his house. Mark didn't even have to find a job.

My brother changed during his senior year in high school. He and I had been so close…he even referred to me as "My Sister the Saint" because he said I never did anything horribly wrong. Then Mark met a guy named "Mitch" who did drugs. As far as I knew, Mark had only smoked a little pot and drank beer. I believe Mitch introduced him to Quaaludes and cocaine. Mark also started drinking a lot and developed an alcohol problem. He was working for our father during the summers, traveling with him on the road as a stagehand and learning about lighting, until Shirley had to fire him because he was showing up late or not showing up at all. He went back home and goofed off.

Mom had a rule: If we went to college, she'd happily support us. If not, then we needed to get a job. We couldn't just live at home and do nothing. So Mark moved out and got an apartment with Mitch. Mark had about $15,000 and spent it all in six weeks, then he moved to Hawaii. He stayed there a few years, working at a fish market.

The next thing we knew, Mark was back, living in the Bay Area and planning to marry a woman named Vesi from Tonga. Vesi was very cruel to Mark, always telling him he wasn't a real Davis because he was adopted. She tried to run him over with my mother's Bronco, and tried to trash the car as well. Mark was married to her by this time, but they quickly separated. Then my brother set about the business of getting his life together, and he did, making our parents— and Jeff and I—very proud of him.

I always thought Dad was far more lenient with Mark than he had been with me when I dropped out of Santa Rosa. Why was it so different for me? Why was Dad playing his children against one another? Years later I came to believe that Dad thought it would inspire us.

Well, he wasn't going to let me move in with him, as he had allowed Mark. So be it. Pop went back to reading his papers and I left without really saying goodbye. Then I found a phone and called my mother.

"Why is he being such a jerk, Mom?" I cried. "He could have said, 'Trace, I'll give you one week. Find your ass an apartment and find a job.' But he couldn't even do that."

"Tracey, your father is just as upset as I am that you left school, but I don't understand why he'd leave you out in the cold," she said. Mom called Dad a little later and he told her he wouldn't let me stay because he was afraid I'd never leave, never learn how to be on my own.

I ended up staying with Guy at his godmother's place. She was a lawyer and had her office in a house on Alvarado Street in downtown L.A. There were shootings and muggings every week; you couldn't go out at night. I cursed my father every day I lived there. Within a few days, though, I got a job with Sumitomo Bank. I went back to see my father with the news.

"See, Pop. I told you I'd get a job," I said smugly.

He just smiled. I think he was proud that I had pulled it off so quickly, but he didn't want me to know. I told him about Alvarado Street and he promptly put down a deposit on an apartment in the San Fernando Valley; Guy and I moved in together. I worked for about a year—even got a promotion. I was very proud of myself as I galloped toward my 21st birthday.

I went home to Tahoe in July 1982 to celebrate my birthday. I had just received the first installment of my trust fund from Dad—he had given all three of his children trust funds when we were young, and they matured on our 21st birthdays. With money to burn, I threw a pool party with trash cans filled with beer and wine, and a barbecue loaded with steaks, burgers and chicken. The day couldn't have been lovelier—Tahoe's cerulean sky was cloudless and filled with light.

First thing that morning, the florist delivered 21 perfectly formed pink roses from an old friend, David Hughes. David was the older brother of my best friend in high school, Andy Hughes. Throughout high school, I'd had a crush on David. He was always so attentive, telling me things about myself no one else ever said to me. He told me I was pretty at an age when I so desperately needed to hear it. David thought of me as someone who could be attractive—even though I thought I couldn't be.

My entire family showed up for my birthday, including Dad, who gave me a tree. It was delivered before he arrived. At first, I didn't pay much attention to it until I noticed there were wads of money rolled up on each branch—$450 after I had unwrapped the bills and counted them. The card was from the florist, but this time Dad had signed it himself: "Love Dad."

My father didn't write very much. I don't know if he was embarrassed about his penmanship or if he just didn't like the chore, but he never wrote anything. I guess it all went back to his childhood, and his lack of a formal education. But he was a voracious learner. Pop couldn't educate himself enough, especially when it came to show business. He always said, "The day I stop learning on stage is the day I retire."

All sorts of friends showed up for the pool party, people I hadn't seen since high school. We started in the afternoon and celebrated until after dark. Pop didn't hang around very long, but was there long enough to take a family picture: Jeff, Mark, Mom, Guy, me and Pop. Then he had to get back to work.

The following fall I returned to junior college to finish my sophomore year. I earned an A.A. degree in business administration. Then I was accepted at Cal State Northridge and made the women's basketball team. I plunged into my studies and played basketball with a ferocity I didn't know I possessed. I saw little of Dad and seldom talked to him.

Then one day, Shirley called with an edgy seriousness in her voice. "Tracey, your dad is in the hospital," she said.

"What happened? Is he all right? I thought he was in Las Vegas," I said, a little panic crawling into my voice.

"He was, but he canceled his show at the Desert Inn. He's having trouble with his hip. It had been giving him a little pain for the past few months, so he went into Cedars for tests," she said.

"Oh. Did he fall? It wasn't the fall years ago in London, was it?" Now I was seized by guilt, remembering how I had laughed at him when he fell off the stage.

"We don't have all the particulars yet. But I wanted to let you know and I'll call as soon as I have anything."

Pop entered Cedars-Sinai Medical Center on Nov. 1, 1985. Decades of dancing had worn down Dad's cartilage and now bone was rubbing against bone, causing intense pain and forcing him to limp. It's a dancer's ailment—Liza Minnelli had the same problem. So did Elizabeth Taylor. So after a battery of tests, examinations and observation, Dad was scheduled for reconstructive hip surgery on Nov. 12 to halt deterioration of the ball joint.

He wore his diamond tennis bracelet to the hospital because he never took it off. But his doctors told him it would have to be removed for surgery. "Why?" he growled. "You're doing my hip, not my hand." My father refused to remove it, but once he was out from the anesthesia, his doctors removed it and gave it to Shirley, who put it back on him after the surgery, before he woke up.

Pop was never a good patient. He hated hospitals, hated doctors and especially loathed dentists, something we have in common. When it came to any type of dental work, Dad would make his dentist put him in a hospital under a general anesthetic before he would allow anyone to touch him. Such are the perks of the rich and famous.

When I went to see him at Cedars, I found out that he had injured himself while working on Irwin Allen's TV movie *Alice in Wonderland*. It was a musical version featuring a whole bunch of stars including Carol Channing as the Queen of Hearts, Telly Savalas as the Cheshire Cat and Ringo Starr as the Mock Turtle. As the Caterpillar, Pop had made a bad move while going through some dance steps during rehearsals. He said his hip had been bothering him for months, but he wouldn't stop working for anything.

One day when I visited, a nurse was trying to get him to use the bedpan. Surely she was joking! I heard the commotion all the way down the hall, Pop screaming something about being a "fucking superstar." When I got closer, I heard the rest.

"You're not putting me on that thing, no way, no how. I'm Sammy Davis Jr. I'm a fucking superstar and I'm not getting on no bedpan," he yelled. "Now get me up."

That's my pop! I smiled to myself.

"Hey, Trace. You have no idea what tortures they put you through here," he said, still in a huff. By this time, the nurse knew half of Pop's fit was in jest and she started to laugh. But he got his own way and had the nurse help him to the bathroom.

Dad was determined, as he was about everything he did, and a week after surgery he was walking around on crutches; he left about a day later for home. I guess bedpans can be inspirational. Pop spent some time recovering at home. The first months of rehabilitation were painful for him as his body healed. He went back to work; sometimes he would limp all the way into the wings before a show, but when he walked out on stage, he forced himself to absorb the pain and walk straight and proud. It was vintage Dad: Sammy Davis Jr., the pro, the consummate entertainer who would never let down his audience.

Pop began working more and more, but I saw him as much as I could, while I applied myself to my studies. The minute I told him I was going back to college, he was thrilled. Once I returned to school, he jokingly called me a "professional student" because I changed majors all the time.

By this time, Dad had warmly embraced Guy. He thought we were good for each other and constantly heckled us about getting married: "Are you going to make a decent woman out of my daughter, or are you going to live in sin forever?"

I also was pestering Guy about marriage until one day we went to the mall in Northridge and I picked out a ring. There, in the middle of the parking lot, Guy proposed. We immediately told Pop, and he couldn't have been happier.

"Well! It's about time," Pop said in his best Jack Benny voice.

Guy and Dad became good friends, and Pop began inviting Guy out to Las Vegas for weekends. The two of them would retreat to Dad's suite after his show to watch movies or play Pac-Man on Pop's table top model for two. Both Guy and Dad were basically quiet. They would sit for hours without talking. Pure heaven, as far as they were concerned. I was still in school, so I missed these male-bonding excursions. But I'm glad Guy and Dad liked each other so much.

Dad even included Guy on his Christmas list and began to give him presents. Pop always gave Altovise money to shop for us. One year we had a strange surprise when we opened our presents. Guy opened his and smiled delightedly at the beautiful sweater that lay inside. Jeff unwrapped a dungaree vest that had been worn. Mark opened a polo shirt with dirt around the collar, and my present was a pair of used, out-of-date jeans. We couldn't believe it. Pop was out, so we called Mom in Tahoe. She was as puzzled as we were. Later that day, I worked up my nerve and confronted my father.

"Dad, why are you so mad at us?" I asked.

"What are you talking about? I'm not mad at you guys," he said, somewhat perplexed.

"Then why did you give us those gifts?"

"What are you talking about?"

"Alto gave us used Christmas presents, Pop."

"That can't be true," he said, not believing me.

"Pop, I'm not kidding," I said. Then I brought the three gifts to show him. He examined them and still shook his head in disbelief.

"Are you sure it wasn't like a little gag and there wasn't a little piece of jewelry or something in a pocket? You know, that's something I would do," he said.

"Yeah, Dad, I know you would. But nothing fell out. These are the gifts."

He grabbed them from me and apologized. Pop felt really bad about that. Mom even called him that night and asked him what was going on. I don't know what he said to Altovise, but they had a fight and Dad threw her out of the house. She had to stay in a hotel for a few weeks. I never found out why Alto gave us used gifts, but I did know she had started to drink a lot. She didn't drink when she first got married to Dad, but I guess the pressures of being with a superstar, especially one who rarely was home, perhaps were too much for her.

Graduation day finally approached and, at last, the first Davis would graduate from college!

Two days before the ceremony in May 1986, my father called me from New York.

"Trace, is it important that I come to your college graduation? Because if it matters, then I'll come. If you don't care, then I'm not going to charter a plane. It's your choice."

I was sitting with Guy at my apartment and the phone almost fell from my hand. What kind of question is that? I always thought parents would kill to see their children graduate. It's what they're supposed to do. How could he not know?

"No, that's all right, Pop. It's not important," I said in a small voice. I hung up the phone and turned to Guy. "He's not coming."

"Well, you told him not to," Guy said.

"Yes, I know I told him to forget it. But I know Dad, and

he knew about this. It wasn't like it was a surprise. All important dates are printed on a huge calendar in his office. He knew. He knew. But he called me because something else came along that he preferred doing and he was trying to weasel his way out of attending my graduation. I know him and that's what he did."

I put my head on Guy's shoulder and cried. I thought back to my fifth birthday party and all the Christmases and Hanukkahs my father never called. I thought of all the empty conversations and vacant chairs of my life. Yes, I certainly should have told him graduation was important and I very much wanted him to be there. But I didn't, because by that time, I no longer gave a damn whether he was coming or not. Just one more disappointment in a chain of disappointments.

My resentment had deep, strong roots and it began gnawing at my soul. Here I was, about to receive my bachelor's degree and do myself and my family proud, but I was wretched. I resented my father for so many things and blamed him for my own flaws. But we continued to carry on a fake relationship. He still didn't get it. He was happy I had completed college, but for some reason he didn't think the ceremony important enough. I wanted him to know by instinct that it was important. I would have to talk to him or I would have to toss him from my life. And the thought of all that made my stomach lurch.

Graduation day came and Mom, Jeff, Guy and I went out to celebrate. When Dad decided not to come, I decided not to "walk" for graduation when the dean called my name. I had majored in journalism with a special emphasis in public relations and a minor in sociology. After a few weeks, I went back and picked up my diploma.

I went to work as a producer at an ad agency in Los Angeles. About two years later, Dad announced on national television that he and Altovise were adopting an 11-year-old boy named Manny. Dad was in Vegas doing the Jerry Lewis Telethon and he made the announcement on the show. The next day, my co-workers asked me about my new "brother."

I had no idea what they were talking about. Then my friend Julie Clark called me and also asked me about it. By the time I finished talking to Julie, I was ready to kill my father. I was furious. How could Dad do something as important as that and not tell his children? I snatched the phone and called his office. Shirley answered and I screamed at her to have my father call me back as soon as possible.

"What the hell are you doing?" I shrieked at Dad when he called me back. "How could you do this to us?"

"Calm down, Tracey. What are you yelling about?" Pop said.

"That kid you adopted. How could you possibly think about adopting a grown child?" I was seething.

"Don't worry, he's not going to take any of your inheritances. I'm not setting him up financially," Dad said.

"You think this is about money, Dad?" I screamed even louder. "This isn't about money. This is about you. You're a national figure and here you go to this nationally televised event and make an announcement about our family without telling any of us. The whole world is up on my family and I'm not. I feel like an idiot and it bothers me. I also don't get it. How can you find time to be a dad to a total stranger when you can't even find time for your own children?"

"I don't know why I announced it on the telethon. It just came out," Pop said. Finally, he told me what was really happening.

"Look, Trace, I'm doing this for Altovise. I don't want another kid, but she wants to have a child. Who knows, maybe this will help her sober up."

"Don't be a fool, Pop. First you get sober, then you get a child. It doesn't work the other way," I said.

"Tracey, I owe her this. It just kills me to find her passed out on the sofa or slumped behind the bar. I want to help her any way I can, and maybe this will."

I saw Manny maybe three times after he came to live at Dad's house, and I may have said 50 words to him the entire time he was there. We don't know whatever became of him, but I do wish him well.

Chapter Ten

It was a week before my wedding and I was a little edgy. Actually, it felt as if someone had gut-punched me, I was so nervous and keyed up. I wasn't apprehensive about my impending marriage, so that wasn't the problem.

The issue, I knew, was Dad. All these years I had carved a monument of resentment. I disliked him for never being at home when we were growing up, for treating us like second-class citizens to his career, to his stardom. I had spent my entire life fighting him. I was always challenging my father's every move and trying to make things go wrong just to get back at him. As I was about to start a new chapter in my life, I wanted to make sure I could go forward without any unresolved concerns from the past.

Now I would have the opportunity to talk to him. Julie and I were going to Las Vegas to spend a weekend at the spa. Pop was appearing at the Desert Inn. Julie encouraged me to resolve things with him, but, oh, did I hate the idea of a confrontation with Dad. That's what was eating away at me, the realization that I would face off against Sammy Davis Jr.

I managed to forget about the talk and have a good time with Julie and Dad. We went to his show and Pop was dynamite. Later we ran over to the Nugget to see Frank Sinatra after his show. Frank had a little party in his dressing room and toasted my marriage to Guy. When we went back to Dad's suite, Julie discreetly disappeared and left me to my destiny. This was the hardest thing I had ever done in my life. I finally worked up the nerve, swallowed hard and said, "I love you, Pop, but I've never really liked you."

I felt an enormous relief, just getting out those few words, a simple truth from my perspective. But my father pulled the rug out from under me and said, "Well, I have news for you. I've never really liked you much, either."

His words sucked the breath from me. I was struck by the realization that I had hurt him as much as he had hurt me. Fortunately, we both loved each other and that's what guided us that night. Love, and honesty. Pop poured himself a Strawberry Crush and sat down beside me on the sofa.

After all my mental agony, though, I didn't know where to begin. So I jumped on something that had happened not so long ago.

"Dad you weren't there for me. I could go back almost to the beginning of my childhood, the part I remember, anyway. But my graduation...let's start there. I needed you there, Pop."

He looked at me quizzically and asked, "Why didn't you tell me?"

"Because I was too scared to say anything. Because I thought you'd know that you should attend your daughter's graduation. Why did you call to find out if you should come? The question you should have asked was, 'When is the ceremony?'" I said.

Dad looked at me in a crumbled sort of way. "I screwed up, didn't I?" he admitted.

I nodded, but I didn't want to punish him. Nor did he want to punish me—that wasn't the point of our talk. "I'll be all right," I allowed. "It's not the end of the world. It was important to me that I pick up that piece of paper. But it's more important for my inner strength that I graduated. I'm happy that I completed my courses."

"Yeah," Pop laughed. "I was wondering if you were just going to switch from career to career."

"But, Dad, how could you not know that going to your

daughter's graduation was a big deal?"

"Yeah, I know. I was an asshole. I knew it was important but I figured if it really meant something to you, Trace, you would have told me to come."

I guess we both were right: He should have known to be there and I should have been able to tell him how I really felt.

I thought of all my missed triumphs; certainly my college graduation was one. Dad went back to the bar, grabbed a Coke for me and poured another Strawberry Crush. He was addicted to that soft drink after giving up alcohol a few years earlier.

Dad had a liver problem caused by many years of drinking and overdrinking. He always had a drink. I never saw him drunk, but he consumed a lot of bourbon and Coke. Just thinking about it brings back that familiar, almost sweet smell of bourbon. He began to get a little beer belly and he was kind of proud of it. We would all tease him about it and he loved it. Only problem was, it wasn't a beer belly at all. His stomach had become swollen because his liver had practically shut down and was moving at a snail's pace. His doctor hospitalized him and told him if he didn't stop drinking he would be dead. So, whammo! Pop quit booze. Cold turkey, just as he had stopped using drugs years before. He still had a small glass of wine every now and then or maybe a beer, but Strawberry Crush was the definite drink of choice.

"Tell me something, Pop, did you know how much I loved basketball and how good I was?"

He shook his head. "Not really."

"I was always upset that you never witnessed all of my little accomplishments, however minuscule compared to what you had done—you never witnessed any of them. That really hurt," I said, biting my lip. Pop swallowed hard and took a swig of his drink. "I could never look up and see my dad in the stands when I was playing basketball. I'm just mad at you. That's all. I'm mad that you weren't there for me on a regular dad basis."

My voice had risen a little bit. I guess I felt on a roll

and everything was tumbling out faster than I knew how to control the words.

"Well, I couldn't be a regular dad," Pop said with conviction, little puffs of smoke from his cigarette trailing his words.

"I know, Dad, but you could have tried to find out."

"You're right. You're absolutely right. I wish I would have. But one thing you should know, Trace—I always was proud of you. Your mom kept me informed about what you guys were doing. She never stopped talking about you. I was proud. And I want you to know that one reason I didn't come to any of your games was because I was worried people would be more interested in me than the team and I'd be a distraction. I didn't want to do that to you."

"Oh, bullshit," I said. "You still could have tried."

He smiled.

Despite their divorce, Mom had continued to talk to Pop about us. But she pulled more than her load and I told Dad that was very unfair of him to make her both our mother and father. He laughed a little and shook his head.

"Believe me, I feel worse about your mother than I feel about anything," he said. "That was my biggest failure. She never did anything but be a great mom and a great wife. I wasn't ready for that. I wasn't ready for your mom, the straight arrow, who didn't do drugs, who was just perfectly content with herself. I needed to run around and be crazy. So it didn't work. It had nothing to do with your mother. Today I'd marry her, because today I don't care about any of that shit that was so important then. Today, I'd be happy."

And he would have been because that was their relationship. He liked just hanging around the house, having a few friends over. Mom liked that, too. She just didn't like all the partying and the wild stuff.

"You know, Pop, when you told me you were marrying Altovise, it was very hard for me," I said.

"I understand that," he said evenly, "but you wouldn't give me an inch. You wouldn't give her an inch, either."

It was my turn to swallow. He was right. I had been totally unfair at the beginning. I always expected he would mess up again. So it became even harder for him to try with me because I was just waiting for the next disappointment, which always came.

"I liked Alto in the beginning, Dad. But once she started drinking, she was mean."

He said, "I know. I know."

"Why did you stay with her?"

"Because I didn't want another failure. I failed your mother, I failed you children. Besides, I owed Alto because she didn't leave me when I was doing drugs and maybe that's how she got started on alcohol."

I told him he could still get a divorce. He laughed and sat up straight.

"What," he almost shrieked, "and give up half of what I have? I worked too hard, too long. Who cares if she's still around? I can do whatever I damn well want to, anyway. You know what I mean?"

"Yeah," I laughed, "I sure do. You always did whatever was important for Sammy Davis Jr. You came first, and that was that. I mean, even now, you only talk to us when we call to check in or when you see us for vacations. You never ask about our schoolwork or our friends or...."

He held up his hand and stopped me. "Trace, it has always been hard for me to relate to you guys as children. Then, when you grew up, it was almost too late. I didn't know you guys then."

"Then why the hell did you ever have us?" I blurted out, tears squeezing in the corners of my eyes. He put his hand on my shoulder and kissed my forehead.

"Because I always wanted children," he said. "I wanted them for all the right reasons, but I never was sure how to go about it."

"Pop, we always felt we had to understand you, but you never had to understand us. Does that make sense to you?"

"Yeah." Dad's voice was growing raspy. I guess it was

scratchy because he was trapped in the same emotional sea as I was.

"Trace, I didn't know how to be a dad," he said almost in a whisper. "I wanted to be a father, but I guess I didn't know where to begin. I just wasn't prepared. I was raising you the way my dad raised me, only I was on the road with him all the time."

What he said made sense to me and helped explain so much. It was like, "You'll see me when I'm on the road, and when I can fit you in, I'll fit you in. When I can't, play among yourselves." I'd always wished my father had been able to understand what kids wanted, what teenagers wanted. But how could he? He'd worked and worked and worked and never stopped working. Being on stage was as much his life force as a heartbeat. The only thing Granddad ever gave Pop was his love when he was growing up. They were on the road, poor and black.

There were nights when Granddad and Will Mastin drank hot water and gave my father a plate of eggs to eat, because that's all they could afford. My grandfather sacrificed for his son and raised him as best he could. Maybe that's why Dad was always showering us with money or lavish gifts, and constantly buying himself things he couldn't possibly use. That was his way of making up for all those plates of fried eggs and mugs of hot water. All I wanted was the eggs...and a little love.

Until that night, I had never had any philosophical or deep conversations with my father. Until then, it had been pleasantries, incidentals, idle chitchat. I got up, stretched and felt my stomach untangle for the first time in hours. I felt as though I was opening up to a stranger. It was the oddest and scariest of feelings. It also was exhilarating.

I reached for a tissue and blew my nose. "I know how difficult I was as a kid. I never made things easy for you, did I, Pop? I never went along with the program."

"Tell me about it. You remember peeing on my lap at Ciro's?" We both laughed.

"I just always felt you were screwing us over when we

were little," I said. "I didn't have the guts to say it then and damn, I barely have the guts to say it now. But I just couldn't act like I was all happy and say, 'Yahoo, we're here with Sammy Davis Jr. Isn't that wonderful?' I just didn't give a shit whether you liked it or not. That was my little bit of power as a kid."

Pop didn't say anything for a while; he was sifting through thoughts. Then he spoke: "You did everything you could to make every occasion hard or difficult. You always destroyed any good time we could have had together."

He reached over and held my hand. I started to cry. "Oh, Pop, I'm sorry. I'm so, so sorry."

He squeezed my hand a little and said, "Come on, Trace Face. Been there...It's over. It's all right. Listen, I always loved you, you know that."

Yes, I knew that. If the chips were down, I knew I could count on my father. I blew my nose some more and let my father continue talking.

"You know why I never worried about you, Trace?"

"Why?"

"Because you're exactly like me: You have strength, you're resilient. I never worried that you wouldn't make something out of yourself without my help. I always knew you were going to make it."

"That's why you never helped me get into the entertainment business?"

"If you had asked me, I would have used my contacts to help you."

I don't know why I had never asked. I guess that's what blind hostility does. I was so angry at Pop for so many things, I had been too stubborn to let him know that I needed him.

Early-morning sun began to filter through Dad's suite. I yawned a little bit and took another sip of Coke. Dad and I looked at each other without saying anything. He always had that ability of wordlessly communicating. Dad smiled, and I said, "I know, Pop. I love you, too." We both cried.

My father wiped his eyes and said, "You know, I never

regretted having you or Mark or Jeff. I love you guys."

He put his arm around me and I settled in on his shoulder. Then I guess we were pretty much talked out. It was almost 7 a.m. "You better go get some sleep," he said, kissing my cheek.

I remained a little longer, hugging my father, drinking in the familiar and very welcome scent of his Aramis cologne. "Well," I laughed, "this is normal bedtime for you, huh, Pop?"

"Exactly," he smiled. "I'm gonna do a little cooking, some chicken, and some tomatoes and peppers."

I rose from the sofa to leave. "Thanks, Pop."

"No, Trace, thank you. I feel a lot better, don't you?"

I said, "Yeah. I really, really do." I walked up to our room on the second floor of the suite. Dad called after me: "Trace Face. One more thing. Give me your phone number!"

I beamed all over. He'd never known my number. Never asked for it. Never called before.

I went to my room with a smile, and immediately woke Julie. I gave her a hug, thanked her for prodding me and told her everything that happened.

Around 8 a.m., I fell across my bed and stared at the ceiling with a big, crazy smile. I hugged myself. So this is what it feels like to have a father. Pretty cool!

Chapter Eleven

I awakened late in the day feeling more rested than I had in years. I felt new, fresh, wonderful. I sensed everything was different the minute I walked downstairs for breakfast. For the first time in my life, I actually felt welcomed, that I was an integral part of his life. In a tiny flutter of time, we had grown closer than some fathers and daughters get to be during their entire lives.

Dad had ordered everything imaginable from room service. He wanted to please me, and he wanted us to have a good time eating. He was on the sofa with his newspapers and a cup of coffee, but he dropped everything and ran over to kiss me when I entered the room. There was a tenderness I hadn't felt since I was a baby, when one night Dad came into my nursery and kissed me awake. "Shhh," he had whispered. "Santa Claus is coming to see all good little girls."

I grabbed a few papers and caught up on the events of the world, while we both devoured mountains of food. We ate together like that long-ago morning of smothered pork chops and shared smiles. We ate and read together like an old, comfortable married couple. Then we both started talking at once.

"So what's going on? What are you planning today? Let's hang out together."

It was all so...normal. I felt so warm, so close, like suddenly I could talk about anything in the world with

Dad and we could do anything and everything together. I felt the same way I had always felt with my mother. Normal.

I considered myself lucky to have worked things out with Dad, because I could not have gone on if we hadn't squared it. Talking to my father opened new vistas to me, a whole new world—a world we could explore together.

I left the Desert Inn with Julie after that long weekend feeling like the princess in a Disney movie—I couldn't have asked for a better ending! But now what? How was I going to incorporate everything into my life? I had spent so much time and energy keeping Dad out of my life and out of my heart that I didn't really trust all these new feelings. I was stunned at how easily my heart just opened back up. We had talked alone: no Shirley, no maids, no security, no Altovise, no nothing. Still, I wasn't sure I could trust my father. After all, I never could before.

But I had seen his face the night we talked. His eyes were so honest and open. I could always tell when Dad was fooling someone. This was the real deal. But could he continue to be open and honest with me? Could he treat me like his "kid" even though he didn't know how to treat a kid? Almost immediately, I was vulnerable once again. This time, though, it was all right. I was going to trust my father and my heart.

By the time I got back home, I missed my father and wanted to talk to him, especially about my wedding plans. Shirley and Mom were overseeing things. Traditionally, Dad didn't bother to deal with the details. He had given us two options: We could either have a large wedding and he'd spare no expense, or we could have a smaller wedding and he'd give us the remainder of the money he would have spent as a down payment on a house. We took door number 2.

I had the perfect place for the wedding: Emerald Bay in South Lake Tahoe, the most beautiful place in the world. It looks as if liquid sapphires and emeralds had been poured onto the rocky crest of a mountain and spilled down to form a gleaming pool at the base. A small island rises amid the lushest pine trees, sheltered by an exquisite lagoon and shrouded on all sides by the Sierra Nevada. In the middle of the island are the ruins of a castle, the perfect shelter for a ceremony. Only a wedding ceremony in the Scottish highlands could match Emerald Bay.

Pop was willing to fly everyone in for the wedding and put them up at Harrah's, but it was becoming too expensive and largely inconvenient for many of our guests. Also, Guy thought it was a little overboard—just a bit too romantic for him and most of his friends. So we decided instead on exchanging our vows before the family and a few close friends at Pop's house, then retreating to Nicky Blair's restaurant for the reception.

I called the Desert Inn and got my father almost immediately. "Hi. I miss you," I said.

"Me, too, Trace Face. You get home OK?"

"Yeah, it was a breeze. Anyway, just wanted to see how you were and, Dad, I wanted to ask you something about the wedding."

"Sure. What's up?"

"Do you have any ideas for music at the reception?" I asked.

"Yeah, I might have a notion or two. Let me think about it. I'm still trying to figure out what I'm supposed to do as the bride's father, you know," he said with a laugh.

I laughed, too. "Now really, Pop, it's not all that difficult. You just walk out with me and turn me over to Guy."

"Well, I've been studying my part," Pop said. "I've watched *Father of the Bride* three times."

Spencer Tracy was one of Dad's heroes and I was named after him, but this was too much—my father was studying a movie to figure out what to do at my wedding! I laughed real hard and then realized how endearing it was.

The movie obviously worked, because when my wedding day came, Dad was in top form. And unlike my high school graduation, he was on time. At exactly 7:30 p.m. on June 28, 1986, when the ceremony was to begin, Pop grabbed my hand, looped my arm through his and said, "Come on, let's go. Time to start."

Pop had a lone harpist playing for the guests, who sat around Dad's living room. Jesse Jackson stood in the center of "The Pit"—that's what dad called the sunken part of the living room—with Guy. As we approached them, Pop stepped around my train and stood near Julie while I stepped into "The Pit" to be married. I felt like a princess in my wedding gown.

I had bought it at a shop on Wilshire Boulevard that no longer exists. I could have had my choice of any dress from any store or designer in the world. Before going to the Wilshire Boulevard shop, I'd gone to Neiman-Marcus in Beverly Hills. Unannounced. You don't do that, especially in torn jeans and a sweatshirt. One of the saleswomen—the kind who wears half-glasses on a chain around her neck— took one look at me and shook her head, no, she did not wish to help me. I guess she thought trying to get me cleaned up would be harder than transforming Eliza Doolittle into royalty. Plus, most brides make appointments and go with their mothers, all spruced up. I was with Julie. I had about $20,000 in my pocket and every credit card known to humanity. The saleswoman didn't know I was Sammy Davis Jr.'s daughter and that I had money to burn.

So Julie and I went to the little shop on Wilshire, started combing the racks and then something caught my eye. It was white silk with a short train and a semifull skirt. The bodice was beaded and off-the-shoulders with sewn-on pearls. It was the most beautiful dress in the world. I tried on a fingertip-length veil that was probably the most delicate and beautiful thing I had ever seen. Somehow, after trying on scads of dresses, I stepped out of the dressing room, and this silk dress had turned me into Cinderella. I had found the perfect dress.

Apparently, from the oohs and ahs and smiles as I walked into Dad's living room, everyone else thought so, too. Guy cried when he saw me in it. I carried a bouquet of simple orchids and white roses. And I wore a diamond bracelet, a delicate, beautiful piece of jewelry my father had given my mother years ago. It was my "something borrowed."

I glanced at Pop every now and then as Jesse began the ceremony. I saw my father with his jaw set, a serious but softened look on his face. I knew how much this moment meant to him. When Jesse asked, "Who gives this woman away?" Dad answered, "Her mother and myself." It was so sweet.

After Jesse pronounced us husband and wife, Dad sank into a chair and cried. Only close friends and family were at the ceremony. Everyone else was waiting for us at Nicky Blair's.

My reception was the party of all parties. Everyone danced and had a ball. Danny Thomas danced a slow dance with me and wished me all the happiness that he and his wife, Rosie, had shared over the years. Steve and Eydie were there, as were Lola Falana, Robert Culp, Lindsay Wagner and many other friends.

I had a special bride and groom put atop my wedding cake, which had white frosting on the outside with fresh strawberries inside. I'd made the bakery break apart two sets so the bride would be black and the groom white. Everyone got a kick out of that.

Before cutting the cake, Dad gave a toast: "Thank you, family and friends, for being here at this special occasion for two people I love very much. It's especially heart-warming to see the excellent taste that my daughter has. I would also like to say we all need to show a linkage in terms of family. Sometimes, we take that linkage for granted. I am personally moved by the fact that my family is here, and the people who are the nearest and dearest to my heart, to help me celebrate this occasion. Tracey and Guy, this is your world.... May it always be reflected, as it is this evening, by people who love you very much. Now cut the cake. I want to find out which chick is going to jump out!"

Everyone cracked up, between tears.

Dad was so right about family. Mom was there, as were Jeff, Mark and Granddad. Granddad and I danced together and he told me I was the prettiest girl he had ever seen. That made my eyes mist a bit. He died two years later.

Guy and I only stayed at the reception for a short time even though we were having such a good time. When we left, everyone else just partied on in true Davis tradition.

Chapter Twelve

Never before had I felt so complete, so happy. I drank in each day like a silky Bordeaux, growing heady over the way my life had turned around. Each day was filled with a new-found joy. I was, of course, very much in love with Guy and glad we had finally married. We spent a glorious two weeks in Hawaii at the Kahala Hilton. Dad surprised us by having our room upgraded to a suite above the pool of dolphins, and he flooded our room with champagne and flowers. We thought we were in a fairy tale.

My relationship with my father was now so easy, brimming with excitement and expectation. I looked forward to his calls, as he did mine. We talked just about every day, completely absorbed by the little details that fueled our lives. I found myself asking him for advice about various problems at my office, and he confided in me as well.

Dad and I had become super close ever since our talk in Las Vegas. From that moment, I felt that my life had suddenly snapped into place. So this is what it is like having a father! Having a dad around was so different. It's what I had yearned for all my life; now I had it. Everything about our relationship was now great. I had someone in my corner, as did he. I could count on him and he could count on me. I could call him whenever I wanted and know he'd be there for me, and now he was calling me. I always had that relationship with Mom, but never before with Dad. We were like two silly schoolkids around each other. We couldn't wait to see each other. Every time he had a party or special trip, he'd invite me and Guy.

One night, in September 1987, I got word about something that would herald one of the proudest days in my father's life. Guy and I had dinner at Dad's and he told us the wonderful news: He was to be a Kennedy Center honoree for life achievement. The whole family was invited to Washington, D.C., for the gala ceremonies on Dec. 6.

After everything he'd been through in this country, the nation gave something back to my dad when they honored him at the John F. Kennedy Center for the Performing Arts. I always knew my father was great, but that greatness never meant more than it did when we went to Washington for the Kennedy Honors.

Dad, Jeff, Guy and I flew into National Airport on Bill Cosby's Gulf Stream jet. We had picked up Dad in St. Louis where he was doing the Variety Telethon. A stretch limo met us to take us to our rooms at the Ritz-Carlton. My friend Julie came down from Ohio to spend some time with us.

After we'd checked out our rooms and found Julie, I called Pop in his suite. "They gave us a limo to use while we're here, so we're going out to dinner tonight. Can you join us?" I asked him.

"Sorry. I'm dining with Senator somebody or another... Shirley, where am I going?" I heard him shouting to his secretary. "Anyway, I'll see you guys tomorrow. This is really something, huh?" Dad was trying some of that Sammy Davis Jr. nonchalance, but I could tell by the sound of his voice that he was extremely excited. He was like an anxious kid the night before Christmas.

"Pop, I am so proud of you and so happy. This is something I'll cherish for the rest of my life," I said.

"Thank you, Trace. I don't know what to say, you know. It means so much to me, more than any award I've ever received. It's like I've gone full circle in my life."

"I understand, Dad."

That night, Julie, Jeff, Guy and I went to a part of town in the northwest part of D.C. called Adams Morgan to have dinner at a wonderful Italian restaurant our limo driver had told us about. It definitely was not the type of neighborhood you drive a stretch into, so when we asked the driver to join us he politely declined and stayed with the car. After dinner, he took us on a tour of the city at night. It was icy and the wind gliding off the Potomac River made it even colder, but we didn't care. There was a glory to this city of lights and history.

We stopped at each monument, bundled up like Arctic dwellers, and took turns reading inscriptions. As I read the words at the Lincoln Memorial, I thought of my father and my body began to warm. I also thought of Abraham Lincoln, my favorite president, a man I've always admired and respected. Ever since I was a child reading the presidential encyclopedias my parents had, I considered Lincoln a hero. He freed the slaves. That's how I saw him. Again, simple right and wrong. Over the years, though, as I learned more and read more history, I realized the nuances and political expediences of Lincoln's action. But in my heart, he is still a hero—a man of courage. Now I was standing with Jeff, Guy and Julie at Lincoln's feet, the feet of one of the greatest presidents who ever lived. I felt overwhelmed and got goose bumps reading the inscription on the monument in the frigid cold. I walked forward until I could touch the sculpture. I touched Lincoln's foot. It was a magical moment.

Next was the Vietnam Veterans Memorial, where all of us experienced deeply personal emotions. As I ran my hand over the names, I had an uncontrollable desire to cry. Just putting your hand on that wall and rubbing your fingers over someone's name goes right through you. To think there was so much controversy over that wall and its design is amazing. It wrenches your gut.

The next evening, the Secretary of State held a dinner for the honorees and all guests. The following day, we went to the White House for a gala reception before the special benefit performance at the Opera House at the Kennedy Center.

Jeff, Guy and I rode to the White House with Dad, so we

could walk in together as a family. My grandmother, Elvera, also was there, as was Alto. Tiny hairs stood at attention on my neck and arms as I walked down the red carpet with my father. I dashed a look his way and saw a small tear forming in the corner of his eye. When he was a child, he could not have dreamed of this moment. Now, after being spat upon, threatened, painted white, beaten up, called names and treated like a dog, my father was walking past an honor guard at the special invitation of the president.

He had been the first black man to sleep in the White House as a guest when President Nixon invited him. But this was different. I held my head high and squeezed my father's arm. He squeezed back and smiled. I was overwhelmed by that walk, by the White House itself. The sheer power and richness of history was immense. We went to the East Room to shake hands with the Reagans in the receiving line. Bette Davis, Perry Como, violinist Nathan Milstein and Alwin Nikolais, a patriarch of modern dance, also were being honored.

Bette was terribly weak after suffering a stroke, and had trouble making the long walk. But she was a tough woman and shook off all assistance. During the actual taping of the show itself at the Kennedy Center, I excused myself to go to the bathroom. As I walked in, I saw Bette inside with her aide. I hesitated for just a moment and backed out. I also blocked the door so no one else could go in. I'm not sure what happened inside, but I felt compelled to protect whatever privacy this great woman had left.

The show was taped so it could be televised by CBS on Dec. 30, 1987. Ray Charles sang some of Dad's songs to honor him. A 104-man chorus paid tribute to Perry Como, and Jimmy Stewart, a past Kennedy Center honoree, talked about Bette Davis while her movie clips were shown.

After the show, Dad took a group of us to the Jockey Club. The elevator doors opened to reveal Walter Cronkite, who immediately extended his hand to Dad and told him how happy he was about his Kennedy honor. Cronkite had served as host of the televised show. Dad introduced us; it was so great meeting him, because we had been raised on "Uncle Walter," watching him all the time on the news. He seemed to be the sweetest man.

Everyone applauded Dad as he walked into the Jockey Club, and after we were seated at our table and delivered drinks, we each began talking about all the things we were grateful for in life. Diahann Carroll and Vic Damone were there, as was Cicely Tyson and, of course, the family. It was a very warm and happy evening. Dad said very little. He just sat sipping Strawberry Crush, a permanent grin dancing across his face, a sign that he was quietly enjoying himself and feeling comfortable.

Out of the blue, Guy, who tended to be as quiet as my father, stood up and raised his glass. "I'm grateful, Mr. D., for everything you've done, but most of all I'm grateful to you for your daughter." I was stunned. Dad was stunned. We looked at each other, father and daughter, with tears in our eyes.

A few days after the Kennedy honors, on Dec. 10, 1987, Dad went back to Cedars for a second operation on his hip. The first had been unsuccessful and he needed to receive a prosthetic. They had to make a special artificial hip for Dad because he was not quite an adult size, and a child's size was too small. He was out of circulation for a while, then back to Las Vegas for work, and then a European tour.

Guy and I joined Pop on one leg of the tour, Monte Carlo. It was the first time I had ever boarded a plane actually looking forward to seeing my father.

Michael Jackson—who had been friends with Pop for some time—had hooked up with him when he was performing in Nice, just to hang out with Dad and bask in his talented glow. That's the effect my father had on younger performers. I'll never forget watching Arsenio Hall and Eddie Murphy around Dad. Here were two mouthy guys who always got their two cents in with everyone. But when they came to visit my father, they were humble, quiet, almost reverential. Both of these men respected a man who had been at the top of his game for as long as they had been alive.

Arsenio hadn't had any superstars on his show until

Dad went on. He'd come around to the house a few times with Eddie and finally asked Dad if he'd do it. Pop said yes, but he'd have to ask Johnny Carson first, as a courtesy. Dad had appeared on *The Tonight Show* a trillion times and had been a substitute host for Johnny, plus they were good friends. So Dad called Johnny, who gave his blessings. Dad appeared on *The Arsenio Hall Show*, a late-night gabfest that attracted a younger audience. After Pop's visit, Arsenio had no trouble getting big names.

So now Michael Jackson was caught in Pop's thrall. Dad didn't know if he'd still be with him when Guy and I arrived, but it didn't matter. I was excited just to be in Monte Carlo with my father and my husband. Pop told us to find a way over and he'd take care of everything once we got there. It was my first economy flight to Europe, a whole new experience, to be sure. Guy and I purchased our tickets on something called "the Apex Fare." Pop laughed and teased us unmercifully about it the entire trip, and whenever anything strange happened, we'd blame it on the Apex Fare. One of our bags got lost, so Dad said, "You were probably over the limit. You know you can only take so much luggage with the Apex Fare."

But my mind wasn't on accommodations while I was flying. My thoughts were on all the times I'd flown to Europe to see my father and tried to mess up the trip so I could go home. This time I smiled the whole way, certainly a strange thing for me.

When we arrived at the airport in Nice, we were picked up in a limo by a driver named Jean Jacques, who drove us to Monte Carlo. Jean Jacques was a wacky kind of guy who decided to show us the sights during our trip. He also was the worst driver imaginable, and every time he looked over his shoulder to point something out, we almost went off the road and down the cliff.

He drove us through an adorable little village high above the Mediterranean between Monaco and Nice called Eze. It was a quaint little place of about a hundred people, with stone houses and winding streets, where we later had a wonderful private dinner at a restaurant with Pop and a few other friends. You walk in to a forest of ferns and other hanging plants. In the corner is a huge fireplace with a roaring fire. That night, a pig was roasting. It was August, so it was hot and humid and the fire made it even more uncomfortable. The waiter brought us white and red wine, but Pop wanted something sweet and light, a liqueur no one had ever heard of.

Leave it to Dad. He had a knack for always ordering things not on the menu, and it was not beyond him to order a steak at a Chinese restaurant. He'd get one, too. When you're a star, you always get your way. If a restaurant doesn't have it, they'll make it or rush out for the ingredients. They aim to please.

We stayed at the Hotel d'Paris in Monte Carlo. It is located in a cul-de-sac right next to the famous casino in Monte Carlo. Guy and I had a beautiful minisuite that overlooked the street, while Dad stayed a few floors higher in a suite with a view of the harbor and palace. Each day, they brought fresh flowers that seemed to have been picked along the countryside the day before, filling our room with wild and sweet fragrances.

There's a magic to Monte Carlo, a peculiar magic that comes from wealth and privilege. Every night, people gathered in the restaurant downstairs, a world-class place called Louis XVIII, everyone done up in finery and jewels. The women in Monte Carlo wore diamonds so large they looked fake. They all had their hair styled each day and wore enough makeup to buy out Revlon. It was an unbelievable display of opulence. The dining room at the Louis XVIII was large, with fresh flowers and terrific artwork. The double doors led to the hotel lobby and outside.

Every night, we'd go out to find a crowd waiting in the cul-de-sac for Dad. As soon as we'd appear, they'd applaud and start screaming, "Monsieur Sammieeee! Monsieur Sammieee!" My father loved the adulation, and now so did I. But it didn't last very long because Dad's car would immediately whisk him away for his performance. The crowds would linger, though—Monte Carlo is a city that never sleeps.

During the day, we went to the private beach club. We were the guests of the Nederlanders, the Broadway producers and owner of the theater chain. They had a cabana and invited us to join them. We would lunch each day in a restaurant in a small cove where musicians played steel drums. Behind us was the beach and Prince Rainier's castle.

Guy and I were more adventuresome than Dad, and we went parasailing one day. It was great. Pop thought we were crazy. But then, there were few sports he involved himself in. In fact, he rarely visited the beach club. He would drop by for a few minutes, then retreat to his suite and sit outside on his private balcony.

After one day at the beach, Guy and I returned to the hotel and checked in on Pop. He had just received free samples of Yves Saint Laurent's new fragrance. It was called Jazz and wasn't yet available in the United States. By the end of the trip, everyone was wearing it. I liked the scent, but by the time I returned home I had tired of it. I did like the idea of wearing an unmarketed fragrance before anyone else though. *Only with Dad*, I thought. *Only with Dad*.

My father's mood was wonderful during our stay. He loved Monte Carlo, and it also was the first time the two of us had ever truly enjoyed each other in Europe. He took me shopping and he bought a wonderful shoe trunk from Louis Vuitton for himself. It held about eight pairs of shoes and cost a fortune. He gave me money so I could shop at Hermés and any other store I could think of. When I ran out of money, I would just tell them to bill the hotel—my father would pay for it! At first, I was shy about mentioning his name, but by the end of the day, I had no problem.

Dad gave one of the best shows I have ever seen when he performed for Prince Rainier and his family. The room—where the annual Red Cross Ball is held—is quite large, with an open roof. The show started at 9 and it was, of course, as hot as August can get. Despite the heat, men were required to wear jackets and leave them on. Guy didn't know the rules and tried to take his off. Out of nowhere, someone appeared and reprimanded him! Guy and I sat with Ruta Lee, an old friend of Dad's; Alex Trebek; socialite Lynn Wyatt; and Andrew Lloyd Webber and his then wife, Sarah Brightman.

My father gave a show to end all shows. He decided to sing "Music of the Night" from Lloyd Webber's *Phantom of the Opera*. Dad is a very good storyteller, and he spent some time talking to the audience about the musical. He spoke of the Phantom living in the bowels of the theater and how he hears Christine (a part originated by Sarah Brightman) singing. Then Pop eased into the song. It was lovely.

I looked up to see the stars as I listened to my father's song of beauty. Then Guy kicked me under the table and nodded in the direction of Lloyd Webber and Sarah Brightman. They were crying. Apparently, my father's interpretation had touched them, with the emotion and depth Dad had brought to the piece. When Dad hit the final note, the audience rose to its feet in applause.

Dad closed the show with "Mr. Bojangles." He had a real love-hate relationship with that tune. There were times when he'd love to sing it, but there were other times when he would be absolutely joyous that he had managed to get off stage without doing it. After the performance, everyone went backstage. Dad was speechless. He knew he had given an incredible show. Lloyd Webber began talking to him about singing the role of the Phantom on Broadway at some point. Dad was honored. He loved the musical. He had seen it in London and in New York and knew the work backward and forward. But my father never got the opportunity to tread the boards as Lloyd Webber's Phantom.

Everyone left Dad's dressing room and we all piled over to Karl Lagerfeld's villa for dinner with Prince Rainier and his children, Prince Albert and Princess Caroline. Candles lined the driveway as we edged up a hill to the house. Gun-toting security men rimmed the estate. Karl had set up little tables outside so we could dine al fresco. He met us at the entrance and Lynn Wyatt introduced me.

"Isn't she pretty?" Lynn remarked to Karl.

I was embarrassed, still so insecure about my looks. I flushed deeply when Karl didn't answer immediately. He took off his glasses and put them atop his head. Then he took a step toward me and looked me up and down. Only then did he give an answer.

"Yes. Quite pretty, in fact," he said.

He asked if we would like to tour the house. It had been a gift from the Rainiers. The only string attached was that Karl had to restore it to its original beauty; the villa had been destroyed during World War II and had stood empty for years. The entire back of the house opened with discreet French doors. The lighting inside was soft, with a peachy feel and cast. Each bathroom was used according to the light: He used one for the morning light and another because it had afternoon light flowing through it. Each room had a different theme with large, unscreened windows overlooking the Mediterranean. Pathways led down to a private beach. The house had cost Karl over $2 million in redecorating and restoration alone, and he wasn't finished yet.

I strained to ask questions and attempt some sort of conversation, but I was lost. Then I picked up on something that gave us a common ground. As we toured his house I noticed that music was being pumped into each room. It was Tracy Chapman, her first album. I had it and loved it, but few people in Europe had discovered her yet. I began quietly singing along with "Fast Car" as we walked from room to room and Karl stopped dead in his tracks.

"You know Tracy Chapman?" he asked.

"I'm a big fan. She's great. I love this disc," I said.

"I can't believe you know who she is. No one here knows her. What other kinds of music do you listen to?" he inquired, as we walked back downstairs to the party. I told him I liked Michael Jackson, my father and tons of others. We ended up talking about music for most of the night. At one point, Guy and I told Karl we were going to Paris before returning to the United States, so Karl invited us to have dinner at his home in Paris.

We walked back outside to the area Karl had set up for dinner. He had a series of small tables, each seating four or six people. I sat with Princess Caroline. We dined on fruit, cheese, a brothy soup and fish. The dinner, like everything else, was simple and elegant. So was Caroline.

She wore a long blue satin dress designed by Lagerfeld, her favorite designer. She was so regal and beautiful that I found myself staring at her. Caroline was working on a photography book with Karl, who was an excellent photographer himself. The princess spoke perfect French to Karl and perfect English to me without once rupturing the conversation. She was amazing. At one point she turned to me and asked if I had any children yet. I said no.

"There's no perfect time to have children. You just have to plunge in. Once you have them, you wonder why it ever took you so long," she said.

Then Caroline told me how her kids would drive her nuts at times, but in the end there was nothing better. She also told me how she tried to keep their lives as normal as possible. I could identify with that and she knew that I did. Caroline was great. We talked like old girlfriends about children, child care and being in the spotlight. My life, of course, was nowhere near as complex as hers; she was a celebrity and I was merely the daughter of one.

Guy and I reluctantly left Monte Carlo. It had been a fairy-tale trip. But Guy had never seen Paris and that's where we headed. Dad was supposed to go also, but he had to cancel at the last minute in order to do a few more performances. He told us to take his suite at the Plaza Athénée, but we didn't feel right accepting the offer because it cost thousands of dollars a night. We could have kicked ourselves for being so honorable! We wound up at the Sofitel, then the Hilton, then the Marriott. When the bellman showed us our room, I started to cry. To go from the lap of luxury to this dingy little room with twin beds and pukey mustard-colored bedspreads was too much. We wanted to stay at the Hotel Georges V (George Vee, we called it), which had been recommended by a friend of mine, but no one seemed to know what we were talking about.

Basically, I never really liked Paris. I don't know if it was the people or the city or the fact that I couldn't understand anything on television or could never find food I liked. I did have fun in Paris once with Dad when I was about 13. He took us to the Eiffel Tower; we climbed all over the place and ate lunch there.

But this was Guy's trip and I was honor-bound to tour with him. I took him all over the Right Bank and the Left Bank. We hit the high spots: Notre Dame, the Louvre, the Eiffel Tower. We saw everything, happily ripped off by cab drivers and served by rude waiters, eating food I couldn't digest. Then, one day, I spotted it: McDonald's! On the Champs-Elysées! Some people call it an affront. Me? I was just happy to be able to get a Coke with some ice in it. The French may know culture, but they don't know a thing about Cokes. McDonald's does; I was in heaven.

Later we had a lovely dinner with Eric, an associate of Lagerfeld who designs watches. Eric brought an armload of fabulous CDs for us—a gift from Karl. Eric was our age and from New York, and took us to a wonderful restaurant in Paris, the only one I ever enjoyed. As we were coming home from dinner that night, we ran into a crowd gathered before a beautiful building.

"What's going on?" Guy asked.

"Oh, that. That's the Georges V hotel. It's the coolest place to stay. You guys should have stayed there," he said.

I was so embarrassed. Guy and I laughed the whole way back to our dingy little room at the Marriott. The hotel we were searching for during our entire stay in Paris was just three doors down from us. And it wasn't George Vee. V was French for the number five, cinq, pronouced sank. Talk about ugly Americans not knowing anything about another country's language. I could only blame myself. If I had taken time to allow myself to enjoy my childhood visits to France, I may have been more open to learning the language.

Chapter Thirteen

When Guy and I returned home, we discussed Caroline's advice on starting a family. She was right—there is never a good time. Guy was still trying to establish himself as an actor and I was busy learning the ropes of production. I was also fast approaching 30.

Pop, meanwhile, was a little working dynamo. He had a new movie coming out, *Tap*, starring Gregory Hines. He had a wonderful role, that of an old hoofer named Little Mo. Gregory was so adoring of Dad, and Pop thought the world of the younger dancer. Their respect for each other really showed on screen—they really looked like mentor and protégé.

Now Pop was also busy setting up the "Together Again" tour with his buddies Frank and Dean. Everyone was excited about those guys performing with one another again. Unfortunately, Dean had to drop out because he just wasn't up to the rigors of the tour, leaving Dad and Frank as a duo. What a concert those two senior citizens gave. Here are Frank Sinatra, age 73, and Sammy Davis Jr., age 62, tearing up the stage like men a third their ages.

They played the Greek Theater in Los Angeles, and Guy and I caught them there. The Greek was primed and pumped that night, as if someone had loaded pure adrenaline vapors into the cooling system. Guy and I sat in the first row just about hugging the stage, a stage crammed with more talent than it had the entire year combined. After all,

Milton Berle didn't call my father Mr. Entertainment for nothing, and Ol' Blue Eyes remained the King of Crooners.

Pop opened, walking out on a simple stage with just his orchestra and a glass of Strawberry Crush. He cruised through "This Is My Beloved," "I've Got to Be Me," "Candy Man" and, of course, "Mr. Bojangles." With each tune, the audience exploded. He didn't dance very much because of his new hip, but he made up for it with song.

Then Frank followed with some of his hits: "My Way," "Mack the Knife," "Witchcraft." He was in good form and the audience swooned with delight. Dad joined Frank for a little medley of oldies, and when they sang "Side by Side," they changed the lyrics from "We ain't got a barrel of money" to "We've got a barrel of money." Everyone laughed, including them. Frank and my father had such an easy way with each other, a rapport that comes from years of shared times, friendship, love and respect. They were best friends and truly brothers.

By the time the final curtain fell, Pop and Frank were exhausted. I found myself bathed in exhilaration—I had goose bumps and I couldn't stop smiling. Guy, too, was elated. He was a Sammy Davis Jr. fan from way back, before he even knew who I was. He also adored Sinatra. We scrambled backstage before the crowds and wedged ourselves into Pop's dressing room.

"Did you like it?" Dad asked, his arms folding me into an embrace.

"You were dynamite, Popsicle," I said, all aglow.

The room began to fill with old friends—Sidney Poitier and Gregory Peck were there—and everyone began talking at once. Pop shouted over the din that we'd all go to Chasen's. He grabbed my hand and I grabbed Guy's, and we dashed from the room. It was about midnight when we arrived at the restaurant. We were promptly ushered to the back room, where Frank already was holding forth with Don Rickles and Ed McMahon. We ordered dinner, and plunged right into the party.

Don was in rare form, needling everyone who came in

but especially turning his funny venom on Frank.

"Hey, Frank, why don't you just retire and be put out of your misery, huh?" he chuckled. Everybody cracked up, including Frank. Dad was doubled over.

"What's so funny?" Don protested. "Come on. Retire already so I can kiss your ring, Frank."

This was an evening for friends, the kind of night my father loved best. It was at gatherings like these that he felt comfortable, safe, loved. He, Frank and Gregory Peck talked about the business and old movies, while Guy and Sidney spoke quietly to each other. As for me, I just sat there smiling, considering myself to be the luckiest person in the world, content just to be a part of such a gathering. It was after 3 a.m. when Guy and I peeled ourselves from the table and said goodnight.

"So what did you and Sidney talk about all night?" I asked Guy as we drove home.

"God. Dunno. I was just so thrilled to be sitting there with *Sidney Poitier*," said Guy. I laughed. "Well, I do remember he said something about how happy he was to be getting back to work again. He has that movie with Tom Berenger and something with River Phoenix."

My brother Mark's middle name is Sidney. Pop named him after Poitier, whom he always credited with paving the way for black actors. Sidney got roles when other black actors couldn't, Pop said, and he took a lot of heat as a result. But Dad always said, "Maybe people didn't understand that he was always the 'Super Negro,' the do-gooder who helped the white people all the time, but a man's got to look out for himself."

My father certainly heeded his own advice. He looked out for himself while competing in a world that was not always open to him and for a long time didn't even want him. It's hard to imagine that anyone could come through that without some baggage or some scars. But Dad and Sidney were both big stars and big talents and couldn't be stopped. I often wonder whether Dad would have been as consumed as he was with work and being a success if he had been white. Who knows? All I know is that my father had confidence and that gave me confidence, to try and be better, to always strive to do more than what is expected of me and never get down on my knees to beg for acceptance.

The Together Again tour turned into the Ultimate Event tour with Liza Minnelli, Pop and Frank. It started in Houston at the Summit and ended at the Chicago Theatre in 1989. They also did a special performance at the Forum in Los Angeles to benefit the Barbara Sinatra Children's Center in Rancho Mirage. Pop was real excited about having Liza on the tour.

Guy and I caught them at the benefit at the Forum. Afterward, there was a little dinner for those who had paid $2,500 for their seats. Tom Selleck was there, as were Gregory Peck, Milton Berle, George Hamilton and other Hollywood luminaries. Guy and I sat with Chevy Chase and his wife, who accidentally left a $30,000 bracelet in the bathroom. Chevy found it, so it ended well. After dinner, Pop took a pile of people back to his house for one of his more intimate parties.

Liza caught a ride in our limo to go up to Dad's house. I couldn't keep my eyes off Liza and Dad. They were both still wired from the show, which managed to raise $1 million for abused children. I saw how Dad and Liza looked at each other, how they communicated without having to finish sentences. They were old, dear friends and truly loved each other; they both had grown up in the business and understood a type of life that few could. I allowed my mind to wander and thought to myself what a perfect couple they made, how wonderful it would be if they were married. Then, of course, I grew up thinking my mother and father made the perfect couple. But what does a kid know?

Later that night, Dad was sitting in the breakfast nook watching television. He often left his parties early, slipping out unnoticed to go to bed or stopping by the breakfast nook just to be alone for a while. He looked a little preoccupied.

"Is anything wrong, Pop?" I asked.

"No. I'm just trying to figure out the show. I need to find a song we can all sing as we reunite on stage after our individual solo parts," he said.

I thought a second and then said, "How about 'Just in

Time'? You know, 'Just in time, I found you just in time...the losing dice were tossed...and you came into my life.' Well, you know the song better than I do. Maybe it can work."

"Trace, 'Just in Time' is a great idea. I'm going to tell Liza." Pop reached for the phone and called her at the Four Seasons. He put me on the phone to talk to her about the song. She, too, thought it was a great idea and they put it in the show.

I was thrilled. I was happy I could help my father with his work and delighted because this was the first time in my life he had welcomed my advice about something concerning business. I swear, I was high for a week!

Dad was so thrilled about performing with Liza and Frank. Three old friends. Couldn't be better, he thought. Friendship meant a lot to Pop. He was friends with a lot of people, all sorts of people—Pop didn't discriminate for any reason. I remember stopping by his house in 1982 with Guy and finding one of the most surprising visitors of all. A very pretty blond woman was chatting with Dad. He introduced her. She was Marilyn Chambers, the porn star. She was so normal and really a lot of fun. After she left, Guy turned to me and said, "She has sex on film. Wow. Can you believe it? What a trip."

Everyone loved Sammy Davis Jr., and he always was so hospitable. Take his weekend screenings, for example. Folks would pile over, always casual. Shirley MacLaine used to come in slacks and a sweater or T-shirt. She was always so great. When we were younger and the Rat Pack was in its heyday, she'd drop over and play cards with the guys in Dad's game room. I used to love hanging out listening to their stories: the time Al Green's girlfriend dumped a pot of hot grits on him; how a crazy man leaped on stage once when Nat "King" Cole was performing and punched Nat in the face in the middle of a song, and no one stopped the guy.

Dad would get movies days and sometimes weeks before they debuted in theaters. I'll never forget how he showed *Star Wars* three days before anyone else could see it. Everyone in the neighborhood dropped by, all sitting around on the floor having a ball. After his screenings, people would hang out as long as they liked. That was Pop. His home was always open to his friends. When he was ready to go to bed, he'd simply disappear. You'd be looking for him and then realize he'd pulled a Houdini.

Dad's friends also liked to entertain. Guy and I once went to a party at Elizabeth Taylor's house. It was for a friend who was dying of AIDS. It was a lovely affair and we truly enjoyed ourselves. But all night, we noticed Elizabeth sitting in an isolated part of the room, surrounded by her Uzi-toting bodyguards. Many guests who approached her were turned away. We thought she may have been overwhelmed by the number of guests there, many of whom she really didn't know since it was a benefit. When it came time to leave, Guy and I went over to thank her and say goodnight, but she didn't see us.

Guy and I loved hanging out with Dad. We always had such a good time together, even though it often irritated my husband that some people referred to him as Mr. Davis. When Pop played Tahoe, Guy and I would go see Dad. Billy Crystal sometimes opened for him. Once when he was there, Guy and I came early in the evening and stayed backstage through the dinner show and the later cocktail show.

It takes a while to come down after performing two shows in one night, so Billy dropped by Pop's dressing room after the final show. It was almost 2 a.m., but both Dad and Billy were still turned on. Rob Reiner was there, too. Somehow they started talking about impressions, which led to chatter about movies and TV, which led to the fiercest, dirtiest, most competitive trivia game ever. We had a ball! Pop was a whiz. He loved movies; he'd even get into all the minutiae such as who edited *Lawrence of Arabia*, or who was the costumer for the original *Sabrina*. Dad knew it all. He loved to talk about show biz, whether you were in the business or not.

Dad and Billy were very close. Dad admired the young comedian, and both had a tremendous respect for the institution of show business and the old-timers who had paved the way. They both treasured that and kept it alive through their talks with each other, like stories passed down among families. It was Pop, the old-timer, passing down a story to the kid, Billy.

⌒

In August 1989 I drove up to Tahoe with my friend Diane to spend some time vacationing with Dad. He had canceled his show because his throat was sore, but he hadn't seemed concerned. We'd been sitting in his suite at Harrah's when Diane and I decided to run out to get some spicy wings from the Goal Post. I had suggested them for a late-night snack and Dad thought that sounded real good. Believe it or not, that simple little decision meant something to me because I had never invited Pop to share take-out before. We had wings and beer. Pop was upset about not being able to perform and a strange feeling came over me, but I shook it off. Since Pop had canceled the show, he felt responsible for the performance. So he called his pal Liza, who was headlining after him. She flew in early, and stepped in for Dad. Her clothes hadn't arrived yet, so she performed in a red sweater, jeans and black boots. She was so casual, and she knocked 'em dead—that's a real performer! We all stuffed ourselves on wings, and Pop never let on that his sore throat was anything serious.

When I returned home from Tahoe, I discovered I was pregnant. When I found out, I was practically speechless. I told my mom first and we both cried with joy. Then I drove over to Sony, where Guy was working. He was practically in shock but also very happy. I knew he was under a strain and growing increasingly frustrated because acting jobs were hard to come by. I saved Dad for last. I called and told him I wanted to come over to talk. He sounded a little worried when he told me to come right away. I drove over and we sat in the breakfast nook, just as we had a few years earlier when I'd told him I was dropping out of school. Now I had good news for him.

"Pop, I'm pregnant, man," I said, smiling like the Cheshire Cat.

He almost fainted. He couldn't catch his breath. Then he stared at me as his eyes welled with tears. "Trace Face, that's beautiful."

We sat there holding hands. "So when is my grandchild due? Is it a boy or a girl?"

"I don't know what it is yet, but it should be arriving sometime in April," I said.

"Trace, you have no idea how happy you've made me. And listen, baby, I'm going to be a good grandpa. I want to be a big part of his life. You can leave the baby here whenever you want to, and I'll even learn how to change diapers."

"Whoa, Pop. That's big time. You never even changed my diapers," I kidded.

"No. This time, Trace, I'm going to do the right thing. Hell, I even want to learn how to feed my grandchild."

Pop's face was totally open and bright. He was so excited about being a grandfather and truly looked forward to helping raise his grandchild. I couldn't have been happier. As I drove home to Simi Valley, I thought about how lucky I was, how wonderful my life had turned out to be. Now I was complete.

From the start, my pregnancy was a difficult one. I began to bleed right away and I was ordered to take it easy so I wouldn't have a miscarriage. I spent more time at home than I ever wanted to and less time running over to Tahoe to see Mom or to Beverly Hills to see Pop, who fussed over me like a mother hen.

Guy and I drove down to Dad's for dinner one night in September. Pop was a little more quiet than usual, but his face lit up when he inquired about the progress of my pregnancy. As we were finishing up, Shirley came in and asked to speak to Guy. I knew Dad was still trying to figure out a belated present for my birthday, which had been in July, so I thought Shirley was talking about it with Guy. When Guy walked back into the room, he kept hidden whatever they had talked about. I had no idea. I looked around the table and Pop was already leaping up and pulling me out of the dining room and into the living room to discuss his grandchild's future.

On the way home I kept badgering Guy to tell me why Shirley had called him out of the room. But Guy's a good actor and he kept things light and playful, refusing to tell me. When we got home, he couldn't hold it in any longer. We were standing at the top of the stairs when he took me in his arms and said, "Trace, your dad's got cancer."

I instinctively reached for my belly and grabbed Guy's arm to steady myself. "What did you say? No. Please, God, no."

"That's what Shirley was telling me when she took me away from the table to talk. He has throat cancer," he said.

"I thought you were talking about my birthday present," I said.

"Your dad didn't want to just drop it on you because of your bleeding. He was afraid for you. He wanted me to find a good time to tell you, but there is no good time," Guy said.

"He's going to die," I wailed.

"Oh, no, Trace. He's not," Guy said gently. "They're going to start treatment right away."

"No. No. You don't understand. This will kill him. I know. I know."

I walked into the bedroom. I knew my father wasn't going to make it. I may have had bits and pieces of hope, but I knew the cancer would kill him. It was a feeling I had; I've had other feelings like this and they were always right. Anyone who has ever experienced this type of psychic knowledge understands just how unshakable these sensations are. I had known Guy's sister would die and she did, quite suddenly from lupus. I knew the *Challenger* was going to blow up, and I had seen that jetliner in my sleep just a day before it went down in the Potomac. Now, I had that same feeling again. I certainly didn't want to predict doom for my own father, but the feeling was disturbingly real.

Once I'd accepted what Guy had told me and was able to handle the sheer terror of what lay ahead, I realized that for once my father wasn't weaseling out of responsibility by having someone else give me such devastating news. He knew my pregnancy was in danger and he didn't want to upset me. He also knew how difficult it would be for him to face me and for me to read his sorrow. I was touched by his action, but I also felt deeply for Guy. It was such a terrible burden for him; knowing the depth of his feelings for Dad, he was just as upset as I was.

I thought about me and Dad: We had just found each other. Were we to be ripped apart? I knew it must have been too good to be true.

Sleep was a callous stranger that night. My thoughts collided and my tears flooded the pillow. The next day, Guy and I went to see Dad. I knew I had to be brave for him. Faced with his own grave ordeal, I didn't want him to have to worry about my health and the baby.

I found Dad in his breakfast nook. He looked so full of life in his red sweater as he sat sipping a Strawberry Crush.

He spoke almost immediately, not giving me the opportunity to be emotional. "I'm going to do the radiation for a number of weeks and then this thing should be cleared up." He smiled at me and Guy, then tried to keep things light by making a joke: "And if it ain't, then they're just going to have to do it again," he said with mock authority.

I smiled and said, "OK, Pop. Kick some ass, man." That's something we always said to each other. We both smiled and hugged.

Pop kept the conversation short. He told me he had gone to see his doctor for a routine checkup and to have his throat examined because it had been a little sore for a while. Dad had thought it was just strain or a cold. His doctor found otherwise. At first, he had thought his doctor was talking about someone else when he was told he had cancer. Then he was angry because it had attacked one of his most precious gifts—and his meal ticket. Finally, he just decided that he was going to lick it, and that would be that.

"Is radiation the only treatment, Dad?" I asked.

"No. They can surgically remove the tumor, but there's a chance I'd lose my voice in the process. I don't want to have to hold that thing up to my throat to speak. I guess if I couldn't sing, I'd delve back into acting and maybe do some directing." But I knew my father couldn't deal with having no voice at all.

I smiled at Dad and fought very hard to ignore the sense of dread that had nestled in my soul.

Chapter Fourteen

The baby was doing cartwheels in my belly—poking, kicking, a left hook, a right jab. I loved every movement.

I was five months pregnant and I tended to talk a lot to my unborn child, hoping the baby would hear all my vocal nurturing. Ever since I'd found out about Pop's cancer, much of what I said to my baby was about him. There was so much I wanted the baby to know about his grandfather because I wasn't certain Dad would live to see his grandchild born.

I thought my maternal musings would somehow speed the birth of my child. Maybe the baby heard my words and realized just how special his destiny was. Maybe, through some embryonic instinct, my child knew he was in a race against time and had to sprint to the finish line and meet his grandpop.

I was thinking about my father right then, as I stroked my swollen middle with my hands. I was about to take a bath when the phone rang. Ordinarily, I'd have let it kick over to the answering machine but these days, with Pop sick and all, telephone calls were too critical. And because Dad never ever telephoned me the first 20 years or so of my life, a call from him now was a singular treat.

As it turned out, it was indeed Pop, and I was thrilled. I still wasn't used to his calls and I guess I tended to act a little like a starstruck prepubescent. My heart beat a little faster, I giggled and grinned and always dropped whatever

I was doing to talk to him. Hey, this was heady stuff. I didn't get it as a kid, and now I was in danger of an overdose.

"Hey, Trace Face," he said breezily.

"Hey, Popsicle. How are ya?"

"Great. Just great. Feel a little energized today."

"Well, Pop, you gotta take it just one day at a time, you know. That radiation is heavy-duty and I know how much it saps you."

"I hear you. Shirley told you about the tribute they're giving me, right?" They were honoring Pop's 60th Anniversary in show business.

"Yes, she called a few days ago. I still can't believe it's happening. Sixty years! That's so terrific, Pop. I'm real happy for you."

"Trace, you have no idea what this event means to me, how wonderful it makes me feel. After all this time. Well, I hope you can come, and I'd like Guy to be there, too," he said.

"We're definitely coming, Pop."

"It wouldn't mean anything without you and Guy being there. I'm saving the seat next to me for you."

"That would be great. Is Alto going?" I knew my father and his wife were having problems, and I wasn't sure how that dissension would affect the show.

"Yeah, she'll be there." And that was all my father had to say about that. Alto was drinking again, and he was worried. She hadn't stopped since her brief stay at the Betty Ford Center. He was silent for a beat, then brightened again. "Everybody's coming back to the house afterward for a little food and drink."

"Cool. See ya there."

I beamed, so happy that cancer hadn't snatched any of Pop's zeal for having a good time. Next to performing, my father's second great passion was partying. Now, we're not talking about a little socializing, a little light hanging out. I'm talking about serious, get-down-and-boogie, hang-it-all-out and stomp-through-the-night fun. A good party was like a sacrament to him, and good friends were his lifeblood.

On short notice—or no notice at all—he'd have 20 or 30

people over to the house. And like an Eagle Scout, he was always prepared. Name your poison and he would oblige—by the gallon. Pop's pantry made a supermarket look like a skimpy picnic basket.

I remember nights when my father screened movies and everybody from the neighborhood came—Lucille Ball, Liza, Shirley MacLaine, Lorna Luft, Tyne Daly and her husband Georg Stanford Brown—or people who were just passing through, such as Rudolf Nureyev. We sat in "the Pit." Only certain people were allowed to actually sit there; the seats were reserved. Dad had his spot and I sat on his right with Guy on my right next to Eygie Rhodes. Everyone else had a seat elsewhere in the living room and no one would sit in anyone else's place. Where you sat at Pop's screenings was a matter of tradition: Once you claimed a certain seat, it was yours for life. Lucy sat way in the back in a big leather chair where she held her little dog in her lap. She loved that chair.

Sometimes, I'd sneak a peak at Pop while the movie ran and I'd see him sitting there glowing at me, his love wrapped up in a precious smile. When Dad was diagnosed with cancer, Guy and I spent weekends at my father's house, and there was always a movie. Once or twice I'd glance Dad's way as I usually did, only to catch him lighting up. I couldn't believe he'd still try to smoke cigarettes with throat cancer, but that's the ugly seduction of nicotine. He tried to smoke two times, but it immediately burned his throat, which had been left raw from the radiation.

Sometimes, I'd leave the Pit and hang out in the kitchen with Georg Stanford Brown, eating Lessie Lee's fried chicken and peach cobbler. Sometimes Lorna Luft would retreat to the kitchen as well.

Then there were the times when show people did what they do best: entertain. Stevie Wonder took charge of the piano one night and started singing. No one asked him to; he just felt like it. I stole a glance at my father and saw another side of him: His face carried a warmth with its usual charm and it held something else as well: pride. Pop was proud of this brilliant musician who so gracefully and quietly took over my father's piano and bewitched us with a song. Stevie would be attending Dad's tribute and I know that made him happy.

Pop's parties were the best. He thrived on laughter and good times, and now, he was getting his due. When Shirley told me he would be honored, I started to mist up. Here he was, a man who had been on the stage since he was three years old, finally receiving the appreciation he so richly deserved, from an industry he loved more than life itself. I was flooded with competing emotions—joy, pride and finally sorrow that it had taken so long and was coming at a time when my dad's life was in limbo.

I only hoped he would be physically up to handling the ceremony. He had been undergoing radiation treatments. Fortunately the procedure hadn't made him that sick, but radiation did exhaust him. It also left a bright pink spot on his neck, almost the color of the Strawberry Crush soda he loved to drink. The pigment was completely gone from the area where the tumor was being irradiated. He usually wore turtleneck sweaters to shroud his neck, which was also a little sore.

I hung up the phone and went back to the tub, thinking about what I would wear to the gala. Not only did I want to look nice for my father, but the event was going to be televised nationally by ABC. Boy, did I have a problem. Nothing fit! I was showing just enough that my normal clothes pinched like crazy, but I wasn't full enough to wear maternity outfits, which I truly loathed. So I dashed over to Ann Taylor and found a simple but stunning black suit, the skirt two sizes too big and the jacket my size. Perfect.

Pop cracked up when I told him how I went out and bought a fat suit. I started to chuckle, too. Lately, we'd found so much to laugh about together. Sometimes he'd start to say something, and I'd jump in and add my spin, then Pop would finish up—always it was crazy, off-the-wall stuff. We were like a father-and-daughter Laurel and Hardy or Abbott and Costello...or Davis and Davis.

Then, a few days before the tribute, the laughter died.

Guy and I were renting a house in Moorpark, a small farming community near Simi Valley, one of Los Angeles' many suburbs. I left home that morning in November 1989 for an alumni basketball game at Northridge. Basketball remained the most important way for me to exercise and stay in shape. I was feeling good, five months pregnant but a babe in an extra large sweatshirt, breezing along California roads in my week-old Nissan 240SX. My car still smelled new—that leathery factory odor that perfumes the air the minute you open the door. I loved it, especially because I'd never had a sports car.

The game was a good one, and we "old-timers" easily beat the current crop of players. I was sweaty and feeling victorious, happy that I still had a touch for competition. I was stoked from the win when I dropped by a friend's house for about half an hour before driving back to Moorpark.

It was early evening, just about an hour before dusk when I started for home. I popped Tears for Fears into the cassette player and snaked my way through Tierra Rejada, a winding devil of a two-lane road. I was doing the speed limit—50 mph—and I remember thinking, *That's fast for this road*. I slowed down, and just as I'd settled into 40, I noticed a car coming toward me. I saw the driver turn her face away from the road. I'll never know what was so important that she stole that second to ignore her driving, but in that instant, her car veered from the lane. There was total panic in her face as she tried desperately to overcorrect. I saw her mouth convulse with a terrified mantra: *Oh shit, oh shit, oh shit*. Her eyes were bulging beacons to the horror that lay ahead. In a blink of time, I saw all of that and more: I saw a ton of steel bolting toward my car to crush me.

There was no opportunity to react. I had time only to think, *Please God, don't let me die, don't let my baby die*. Then I closed my eyes....

Drip. Drip. Drip. I heard no sounds but an incessant

and intrusive dripping. My face was wet. Was it raining? No. I was inside, upside down. Inside a car. The car was hurt. The car was bleeding. Car blood? My blood. My stomach hurt. Oh, God, please. Not the baby.

I was disoriented for a second and then, with great clarity, I knew I had to get out of the car. I thought it would explode, killing me and my unborn child. The Nissan was lying upside down on the side of the embankment, a jagged heap of metal and glass. The heady aroma of newness had been replaced by the terrifying odor of disaster.

I was pinned upside down, strapped in by the seat belt. I couldn't get it undone, because I had forgotten the 240SX had the new automatic seat belts that had to be released from the top and not at the waist. I panicked. I was worried and couldn't quite put it all together. I kept thinking I would be incinerated in a burning car. In my hysteria, I almost didn't hear the banging on the window. There was a man, a stranger. He was asking me something: Was I all right? Was I alive? Then he somehow managed to get the door open and free me from the seat belt. After he had pulled me out and propped me against the embankment, he asked for my telephone number and called Guy. I never knew his name and I never saw him again to thank him for saving my life.

I was sitting on the side of road when the police arrived. An officer came over and asked me where the other people in the car were. I assured her I was the only person. Then she said, "Damn. I radioed that we had a fatality. I'll send for the ambulance right away. I thought you were dead."

I was stunned by what she said. I, too, had thought I was dead. But I couldn't die, not then. I had Guy, and a baby coming and there was Mom and, of course, my dad. Oh, Pop. *God, someone has to call him,* I thought. I worried about that—he was under so much stress from the cancer treatment and preparing for the special. I didn't want him to be upset.

Guy arrived while my thoughts were still tumbling

about. The street was completely blocked off and he ran right by me—he didn't see me. His focus was on my car, lying on its top in a ditch. I was being loaded into an ambulance by the time he found me. He told me that when he'd received the call, he'd thought someone had rear-ended me or I'd been in a fender-bender.

"All I could think was, *Tracey's gonna be pissed. Her new car!*" He told me this with tears in his eyes, but he made me smile.

I was hurting real bad by the time the ambulance got to Los Robles Medical Center in Thousand Oaks. There was a stabbing pressure in my abdomen. I was terrified I was having a miscarriage. The attending doctor in the emergency room checked me out while I yanked out the shards of glass that had become embedded in my hair. The doctor called my obstetrician and after much debate, my OB decided I could see him in the morning. I didn't tell either doctor how paranoid I was about riding in a car; at that moment I truly thought that if I got into a car again, I'd die and so would the baby.

I was choking on tears and very, very afraid. I felt small, like a child, vulnerable and unsafe. I was so thankful Guy was there. But more than ever, an invincible truth pressed on me like no other: I wanted my father. It was a need I had felt several times, of course, but always pushed away because I expected he'd disappoint me. I'd always needed my mother, and I'd always known she was there for me. She was in Tahoe now and I knew she'd feel frustrated that she was so far, so I figured I'd call her about the accident once I got home. Dad was only 45 minutes away. And my need for him coursed much deeper—I had to feel his concern, I had to know it existed. Maybe I was being selfish; maybe I was just allowing myself to believe for the first time that he would not disappoint me. Whatever the need, it felt so natural, so real, to just let go and trust in his love for me.

I told a nurse to call my father.

"What's his name?" she asked.

"Sammy."

"Sammy what?"

"Sammy Davis Jr."

"Ooooooh. Not *the* Sammy Davis Jr.?" she gushed.

"Yes, that's him," I said, as my sobs subsided.

"I'm such a big fan of your dad's. Will he come to the telephone?"

"I don't know," I answered honestly. "But just tell whoever answers the phone that his daughter is in the hospital."

"Oh my God. Oh my God. Are you all right?" Dad was beside himself. "Can I come out there? Are you sure you're all right? Is the baby all right?"

Dad was in a panic. He wanted to do something right away, so he told me not to worry about any hospital costs; he'd take care of everything. This might sound strange, but it was kind of nice of see him so upset. This was the first time in my life I'd ever seen my father really emotional—about me, about something he really couldn't help. I felt oddly happy, despite the pain, despite the terror of the accident and fear for my baby's safety.

One of my major peeves with my father before we talked to each other and straightened out our relationship in Las Vegas had been that he had no idea of how to reach me. He never knew my telephone number and he didn't know my address. Oh, they were written down somewhere with an assistant. But Pop couldn't pick up the phone himself and call—I wasn't even on speed-dial! It used to make me mad. If I was out somewhere, had an accident, was unconscious and someone found his name and number listed as the emergency contact and called him, he wouldn't be able to tell anyone where I lived. He wouldn't have a clue.

"Look, I'm on my way. I'll be there in less than an hour," he repeated.

"No. It's OK, Pop. I'm going home in a little while." Then I started to cry again. "I just want the baby to be all right, Pop, and no one is telling me for sure if it is."

"Honey, I think you should stay the night there. I'll come over," he said, his voice scratchy.

"My doctor said I could leave. Guy's here. I'll be OK." I don't know who I was trying to convince more, Dad or myself.

"Well, put Guy on the phone," Pop said. "I'd feel a lot better if you stayed and made sure everything was all right. But you call me the minute you get home." There was a catch in my dad's voice. It was something I never heard before, not even at my wedding ceremony: He was nervous.

My father was gravely concerned—just like a regular parent! It was weird. I didn't need an accident to know my father loved me and that I loved him, but life-threatening crises reinforce fragile bonds. My car wreck gave us more of each other and reminded us of what truly mattered in life.

Going home that night was scary. It was pitch black and extremely foggy by the time Guy put me into his car. The visibility was zip and I was terrified. We couldn't see a thing. Guy kept yelling at me to close my eyes and I did. I traveled like a blind person and was grateful for the oblivion. To my relief, I managed to stay alive during the ride home.

The phone was ringing when we walked through the door. It was my father. Not someone else calling for him, as always had been his practice, but Pop himself.

"How do you feel, darling?"

"I'm in a little pain, Pop. My face is pretty cut up, and there's still some glass in my hair and scalp. My legs are badly bruised, my shoulder is badly twisted and my back is messed up. And God, I'm tired. But I'll be all right, Pop." Then I started to cry.

"Ah, my Trace Face...." Pop let me cry for a bit. "You're going to be just fine. You just got shook up a little. But be sure you get yourself and the baby checked out by your own doctor tomorrow."

"Yeah, I know. I'm gonna do that. But Pop, it's just that

I know I won't be able to make the tribute. I'm in too much pain and too banged up right now."

"It's all right. Forget about it. There will be other specials. You can count on it. Listen, put Guy on the phone. I have some good news; I want to tell you both, together." He waited a second for Guy to pick up the other line. "The cancer is gone."

"Yahoo," I screamed, not really believing what I was hearing. But Dad's good news that the radiation had been successful helped diminish my guilt at not being able to attend his tribute.

His doctors had given him two options after discovering his cancer. The first was surgery to remove the cancer. But this procedure carried a big problem: There was no guarantee Pop's voice box would be left intact; he might have to wear one of those devices pressed against his throat in order to speak, something that would have made him the Dr. Strangelove of the Rat Pack. Even though he had a 7 in 10 chance for survival, there was no way Sammy Davis Jr. would go for this. The second option was radiation, with a survival rate of 2 in 10.

I never understood why he would not choose the best weapon to save his life. He was going to war with a water pistol when he needed an Uzi. He had always been a fighter. Why not now? Was he giving in? After a while, I learned to accept his decision to have radiation because I gradually realized that life is defined in many ways. For Sammy Davis Jr., his voice was his life. Lose it and you lose him.

Still, a small part of me always harbored a pocket of resentment toward the radiation, and complete anger at cancer itself.

Dad called every day after the accident, several times a day, and I phoned him at least as much. He offered to come out to Moorpark to see me, but I kept telling him there was no need. It was the first time my father had ever offered to visit me. He had never seen a single place I'd ever lived in as an adult. I had always gone to see him and he'd never wanted to come to me.

The tribute was held two days after the accident. I told Guy he should go, that there was no need to stay with me. But he said he'd stay at home with me. Jeff and Mark were there and Dad was so happy.

Several weeks later, Guy and I went to the towing yard to see my car. It was totaled. All that stuff the salesman had said about the crumple zones was correct. The Nissan had saved my life. It had rolled and the top didn't cave in, even with the sun roof. The new seatbelt system saved both me and the baby. The automatic shoulder harness had kept me in place, and I hadn't worn the lap belt—it had to be done manually and I always forgot to put it on. If I had had it across my belly, the baby might have been crushed. By all accounts, the crash should have killed me.

Three months later, Guy and I watched the tribute on television. It was quite a show, boiled down to two hours from more than two and a half. Pop sat in the front row with a permanent expression of joy and love on his face. Eddie Murphy was the host, and all of Pop's pals performed: Frank, Stevie, Cos, Whitney Houston, Michael Jackson. Liza was there, and Gregory Hines, Goldie Hawn, Clint Eastwood, Shirley MacLaine, Dean.

Frank was in tears—and he wasn't alone—as he talked about the decades of friendship he shared with Dad. I still remember his words: "You're the best friend I ever had....You're my brother."

Pop hopped up on the stage and tapped a bit: A smidgen of the old energy was back, enough so that Gregory Hines bent down and kissed Dad's shoes.

President Bush detailed my father's humanitarian efforts—his incredible support of black colleges, the NAACP, AIDS causes, Israeli causes and other social issues—and there was a special clip of Ronald Reagan hosting *General Electric Theater*, the episode when my father made his dramatic TV debut in the 1950s. That was my pop, and was I proud. At the end of the show, Dad held a press conference and announced that the tumor had disappeared, that the MRI showed no evidence of cancer.

Everyone was so happy for him, even jaded reporters and gossip columnists.

The show was a one-of-a-kind TV special, not the usual smarmy variety hour. This was a show about friends supporting and acknowledging one of their own. It won an Emmy award in September 1990 for best variety, music or comedy special.

There was a party, of course, at Pop's house after the tribute where something lovely happened. My mom opened the door to Dad's office to say goodnight and found my father praying with Jesse Jackson and Michael Jackson. They were thanking God for taking care of Dad, for the remission. It was a private and beautiful moment.

I still feel pretty bad about not being with him that night. Could I have gone? I couldn't have. I was hurting too much and there was the baby to think about. I think Dad understood, but I'll always feel the ache that comes when a treasured moment tumbles from your grasp for all time.

Pop was wrong. There were no more anniversary specials for Sammy Davis Jr. Had I known it then, I would have gone, taking whatever drugs I needed to get me there and lying down the entire way in a limousine. Anything. Just to be there.

Chapter Fifteen

The cancer had not gone away. It had always been there, stealing through my father's body like a murderous thief. Remission had been but a tease, playing with our hopes and spirits, setting us up for a terrible fall. Hope was the great missionary, especially after Dad had almost died the first time he was hospitalized. He got better, but now there was a more ominous feeling because Pop had developed an infection after oral surgery that rapidly sped to his lungs. A thick, mucouslike substance flowered and threatened to choke him.

It was all so fast: One day he was a bundle of energy, heady on the MRI report; the next, he was a fallen man, cowering before one of God's crueler mercenaries.

My nerves were still jangled from the car crash. I was devoting much of my attention and strength to healing myself and just safely getting through the pregnancy. So when Shirley called me that day from the hospital to tell me my father was stricken, I was not prepared for what lay ahead.

I went to see Dad the day he re-entered Cedars-Sinai. As the hospital elevators opened onto his floor, I was immediately assaulted by that "smell"—that sour odor of unwellness you get only at such institutions. I hate it, that combination of medications and illness. I had smelled it when Peewee was dying in a different hospital years before. Guy gave my hand a supportive squeeze as we started the long walk down the hall to where my father's camp had been set up in two rooms.

Dad was not the only famous person in Cedars at the time. Pop's buddy Dean Martin was in for a few days. And Charles Fleischer, the voice of Roger Rabbit and other animated characters, was there, as was Billy Idol. As sick as they were, they all found time to send their prayers and good wishes to my father.

Sarah Vaughan was also a cancer patient. Everyone thought she'd survive chemo and make it, especially her daughter, Paris, whom she had adopted at birth. Paris came down to Dad's room a few times to visit, and she and I wound up in long conversations about the downside of having famous parents. Paris is an actress but she wasn't working very much at the time. She told me how difficult it was trying to measure up to her mother and be a success. She always sought validation from her mom, just as I always sought affirmation from Dad.

It was so important to me for him to know that I was good at something, that I did indeed have a natural talent. And one thing I longed to be was an actress, but my school didn't have a drama department—and I was paralyzed with fear. I didn't want the ridicule: I would always be compared to Sammy Davis Jr., and they'd be lining up to rip me to shreds. I could just read the headlines: "Sammy's Kid Bombs Out." I couldn't take that type of criticism. Paris understood. She, too, walked in her mother's shadow.

I grew up feeling a little annoyed that Mom and Dad hadn't given me a nudge into show business. If they had introduced me to the stage when I was little, maybe I wouldn't have been quite as fearful of failure. I'd been quite the little show-off when I was younger. That's one of the things I discussed with Dad in Las Vegas—I told him I was serious about following him and Mom into show biz. I should have been another Jamie Lee Curtis or Natalie Cole.

"I didn't think you had any interest in it," he'd said.

"Pop, you never asked."

He said there were a lot of things he'd never asked

Mom and Dad shortly after they brought me home from the hospital.

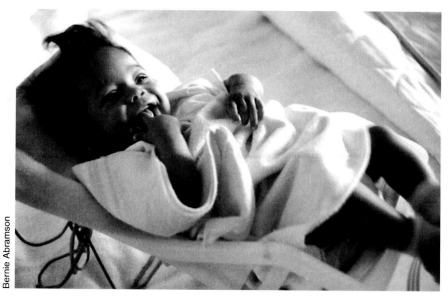

Bernie Abramson

Me at four months old.

The Davis Family Collection

Dad giving me a hug and me not quite sure how to react. I was a pain in the butt even back then.

The Davis Family Collection

Mom and me when I was four years old. Despite everything, my mother was a saint. You couldn't ask for a better mother and I only hope I can be the mother she is.

Mark, Jeff, Mom and I in Las Vegas. Although my parents were divorced, Mom sometimes traveled with us.

Dad in Washington D.C. the week of Martin Luther King's "I Have a Dream" speech.

Pop and me at his Beverly Hills house astride the car I would later drive.

When I told my father I didn't have any good pictures of him, he autographed this one as a joke.

Dad and I at my wedding reception in Beverly Hills. We didn't know this was being taken but I love the look on my father's face.

My mother, Guy, me, Dad and his wife Altovise. Guy hated this picture because of his hair. But I love it because Dad was cursing through his smile. We were all cracking up. It was hilarious.

My brothers Jeff and Mark flank Dad at my wedding. This is probably the best picture that exists of the three of them. It was a spectacular evening.

This is the only picture of Guy and I that I like. It was taken in 1994 when Guy was getting new head shots. I slipped in between rolls of film.

Guy and Sam outside Miss Debbie's room on Father's Day at Sam's school in Woodland Hills. My father never made it to one of these. I cherish this picture with all my heart.

Our daughter, Montana Rae Garner, age 2 1/2, in the car with her blankee wrapped around her. I love this picture. She looks so beautiful and mysterious.

about, and I said, "You're right!" But when I was younger, I'd never felt comfortable enough with Dad to have him teach me stuff and work with me.

Now as I walked down the hall at Cedars-Sinai, acting— for all its allure—was the most remote thing from my mind.

Shirley (whose bandleader husband, George, had died just a few years before) was doing a remarkable job of holding things together at the hospital with Murphy Bennett. George, Shirley and Murphy had worked for my father for 30 years or more apiece. Whenever anyone arrived at the hospital, either Shirley or Murphy would slip into my father's room to find out if he felt like having visitors.

But this day was different. There was no one in the outer waiting room. The absence sent a prescient chill through me. I knew Dad was sick and I was about to find out just how sick he was.

As Guy and I reached Dad's suite, Shirley almost immediately came through the door, rubbing her crimson-rimmed swollen eyes. She looked at me without speaking, and I blurted out point-blank:

"Shirley, is my father going to die?"

Her answer was simple and direct. "Yes."

I felt as if she had punched me in the stomach and knocked the wind from my lungs. I couldn't breathe. My knees began to collapse and I began to taste the sickly hospital smell. I wanted to vomit, but Guy grabbed me and propelled me around the corner, where we found a small, impersonal haven in the hallway.

My sobs came like hiccups, and somewhere in the distance I heard Guy's. We stood like two wind-up toys, broken and propped against the wall, a wailing wall. We were together but we couldn't hold each other. Guy and I were each going through a private hell and, for the moment, we were each on our own.

A lifetime later, I dried my eyes and made my body move back toward my father's room. I would have to face him but I had no idea how. I couldn't even begin to envision what it would be like, what to say, what to do. My mind was numb and wouldn't focus. It was somewhere I didn't know, lost. I felt lost, too, like a little girl at the shopping mall suddenly separated from her mother. And scared. Really scared.

As I drew nearer to the room, my mind returned from its trip and began feeding me happy images of Dad: I saw him smiling, his body folded over, laughing with his eyes closed; I saw him hugging me on my 21st birthday when the whole family got together at Mom's house in Tahoe. I saw my father through little-girl eyes: I was three, sitting on his lap at Ciro's in New York; I was five, invading one of his business meetings in Beverly Hills. I had never called him Daddy, but that's the name my mind now screamed so sadly.

Guy let me go in alone to see Pop. I had to—that much I knew.

The room was incredibly hot, just the way my father liked it; winter or summer, it didn't matter. I remembered how Mark, Jeff and I used to laugh whenever new people came to see Pop: They'd squirm from the heat. We, of course, knew to always dress in cool clothes. I smiled at the tiny figure in the hospital bed, thinking of the heat torture he put so many people through.

I was amazed at how small my father looked. His breathing was heavy and labored; it seemed as if he had tubes coming from everywhere. He looked just awful. As for me, I looked fat and pregnant in sweatpants and T-shirt.

I sat by the bed facing the window. The sun's rays burned through the flimsy institutional curtain, heating my face, while the cheap vinyl from the chair threw off so much warmth they made my thighs stick to my sweatpants.

Dad was staring at me with one of those looks that say so much. I looked at him through watery eyes, my mouth puckering as if I had just eaten a piece of sour candy.

"I know, Dad," I said. "I love you, too."

Shirley and Guy were waiting when I left the room.

"Have you called my mom?" I asked.

"No, I was going to call her later today," Shirley said.

"Please. Let me be the one to tell her." I said. This, too, would be an extremely difficult task. It seems destiny had dealt me one doozie of a hand and there would be no easy outs.

Mom had bought Jeff a video store in Tahoe. She was working there that day, so I called her at the shop. I tried to keep things light and fell into the easy patter of small talk. Then I told her I was thinking of driving up to Tahoe, and Mom could tell from my voice that something was dreadfully wrong. She asked me. I told her it was Pop.

"I think you, Mark and Jeff should probably think about coming down as soon as you can," I said, trying not to cry.

"How bad is it, Tracey?"

"It's pretty bad."

"Tracey, tell me...."

"Mom, Dad's going to die."

My mother let out a low guttural sound and began sobbing. "Oh, my God. Oh, my God. Oh, Sammy."

Mom and Dad had never stopped loving each other. After the divorce, Mom would come to Pop's shows in Tahoe. She'd go to his dressing room, and they would hug and kiss. When she'd leave, he'd say, "Bye, May. I love you." Now, Pop told a lot of people "love you" in that show biz kind of way, but this was special, deeper. I know that if Dad hadn't remarried, they would have ended up back together because they had gone the whole circle and now were ready for each other.

Mom went to see Pop in the hospital, and he brightened whenever he saw her. But her visits infuriated Altovise, whose drinking problem had escalated with Dad's illness. I always thought Alto was jealous of my mother. She knew that Dad still loved his first wife, and that she couldn't stand. Alto also longed for the professional respect my mother had, even though Mom had been out of the movie business for years.

I remember one night we were all at Dad's house and Alto started asking questions about getting into the Academy of Motion Picture Arts and Sciences. Alto had had parts in a few forgettable movies, such as *Kingdom of the Spiders* (a B-movie that starred William Shatner as a veterinarian fretting over killer spiders), but she wanted a little caché. She'd asked Dad what the rules were for joining the academy. Pop had told her you have to have a body of work, maybe four movies.

Altovise said, "Well, I've done four films."

"Yes, dear, but they have to be of some merit." Dad started to laugh and laugh and I joined in, as did everyone else. That was my dad, a real zinger and very funny, sometimes at someone else's expense. But I don't think he was trying to be mean to her; he was just having a little fun.

Pop did love Altovise. I remember how torn up he was over her drinking. He once told me, "Don't you think it breaks my heart to come out here and see her passed out from alcohol, lying on the floor? It kills me." There were times over the years when he'd leave her for periods of time and escape to Scottsdale, Arizona, to play golf. I remember him calling once or twice at Christmas when we were teenagers, telling us he'd be in Scottsdale and inviting us to join him if we wanted to.

But right now Pop just wanted out. When he came home from the hospital, he had Altovise locked out of his bedroom. Not only didn't he want to be bothered with her, but he was scared to death that she would stumble in drunk. "You know," he said, "fall on top of me and kill me because I won't have the strength to peel her off."

Dad pretended he was asleep most of the time when Alto came to see him at Cedars-Sinai. It seems his absence from the house had given her carte blanche to drink.

My father's house was alcohol heaven. Because he constantly entertained, he had more liquor on hand on any given day than most people purchased in a year. Need more? Call the liquor store. No money? Put it on the account. No car? They deliver. It was way too simple and far too seductive for a substance abuser.

Dad wasn't especially good at handling personal problems, so he didn't want to deal with Altovise. Though she had tried her best to adjust, being Sammy Davis Jr.'s wife had not been easy for her. And even though Dad had told Alto before they married that he didn't want to have any more children, I think she longed to have a baby and thought maybe he'd change his mind one day.

Alto had been to the Betty Ford Center before I was married in 1986, and had left—against doctor's orders—to attend the wedding. She never went back to Betty Ford and she never stopped drinking. She once tried to fool my father into believing that she had been going to counseling for over a month. One morning, though, Dad answered the phone. It was a counselor calling to say that Alto hadn't been there for weeks. Another time, Dad confronted her, but she weaseled out of it with some excuse or another.

I once asked my father why he didn't make her sign in at Hazelden for an extended period of time. "I can't do it. She'll have to help herself," he said.

With Dad terminally ill, Alto was even more out of control, and Dad didn't want to come home to that. He wanted to stay in Cedars-Sinai where there was no stress. But we all worked on him, convincing him that he would be happier and more comfortable in his own house in Beverly Hills.

Shortly before my father left the hospital, his lawyer and good friend, John Climaco, had a meeting with me, Alto, Shirley and Murphy. My father was coming home to die. He had a few months left but we weren't sure how many, and we had to put his business affairs in order.

John started the meeting by telling us what we already knew: Dad had a whopping IRS debt. If he had been able to work the rest of the year, he would have been free and clear. Since he could no longer work, the federal tab kept mounting, because the interest rates and penalties the government slapped on would've made the Mafia proud. Dad's tax bill now loomed at roughly $5 million. John ran this by us, adding a few facts here and there. All the while Alto sat, shaking her head in disbelief. She constantly interrupted John and insisted that she had no knowledge of Dad's tax problems.

"You signed jointly on his tax returns," John reminded Altovise.

"I never signed that," she said, shaking her head. "You're wrong."

I snapped. I was so mad I was just about pissing bullets. I turned to Altovise and told her she had a drinking problem and that's why she couldn't remember anything she had done. She denied she had a problem.

"The hell you don't," I said. "Why do you think Dad didn't want to come home? He doesn't want to have to deal with all your shit." Alto just sat there. I inched forward in my chair and pointed my finger at her.

"If you take one day, one hour, one minute off my father's life because of your drinking and the stress it causes, I will come up here and I will *kill* you."

The whole room was silent, but Alto rose from her seat and pressed her face close to mine.

"Oh, yeah?" she challenged.

I didn't budge. "I will *fucking kill you!*" I screamed. "Are we clear?"

With that she backed off. I was trembling with rage and patted my stomach to calm the baby, who must have known Mom was going off on someone. But I don't think I'd been more serious about anything in my entire life: At that very moment, I definitely would have killed for my father.

The next day I went to the hospital for my regular daily visit with Dad. He looked in good spirits, a lot brighter.

"I heard about what happened last night at the house," he said.

I was a little taken aback that he knew what I had said, and thought he'd be furious at me. I started thinking of ways to apologize for being rude to his wife, but I couldn't. I had meant everything I said, and I was ready to accept his wrath. Instead he said, "Thanks. I love you."

We held hands a while before I left to go home. That's when I really knew there was no hope for my father. Because when I got to my car, I rubbed my hand under my nose. Instead of Dad's Aramis, which I always smelled when I touched him, I was assaulted with that unmistakable odor of death. Once you smell that smell, you never forget it. You can pull it out of the air wherever you are.

Cancer stinks.

Chapter Sixteen

My father's homecoming was a finely tuned operation, because sneaking him out of the hospital was no easy task. After all, Dad was still a huge celebrity and the tabloids love a good picture—especially a photo of a star who's dying.

While he was still at Cedars-Sinai, one of the tabloid reporters stole into the hospital to cop a few photos. Dad had been walking up and down the corridors one day getting his exercise, and this bozo snapped his picture. I couldn't believe that someone would stoop so low. He never asked my father's permission and the creep could see that my father was in bad shape: He weighed about 85 pounds, had IV packs attached to him, and his hair was uncombed and spiking up all over the place. He was frail, vulnerable, sick. Fortunately, Dad's security guard, Brian Dellow, managed to wrestle the camera away from the photographer and seize the film.

That photographer was probably among the pack that swarmed outside the hospital the day Dad left for home. News had been leaked that Sammy Davis Jr. would be going home, so it was no surprise they were all clustered, waiting to sprint for that all-important photo op.

Brian, a former Scotland Yard man who had been with Dad for years, managed to spirit my father through a back corridor to a little-used elevator. Somehow, during the few weeks Dad was in Cedars-Sinai, Brian had found hallways and passageways even most hospital personnel didn't know existed. And so my father and his entourage snaked through a warren that finally spit out into a back parking lot where Brian had a van waiting.

The split-level master bedroom suite at Dad's house had been turned into a minihospital. The bottom floor had been Dad's office. Now it was occupied by Shirley and Murphy. They ran his business affairs from there, and the room also served as the place where well-wishers gathered. His room and bathroom were locked from the inside so now no one could have access to him unless they entered through the office and passed Shirley's watchful eye.

The midlevel was the nurses' station, with monitors, life-saving equipment, medication and everything else you'd find in a real hospital. The main level was my father's bedroom and bathroom, which combined were as big as most people's apartments. With my father's specially made king-size bed removed and replaced with a hospital bed, the room seemed even more vast.

All the speech-making to Altovise didn't do any good. She was drunk when we arrived home with Dad. I gave her a murderous glare. Dad just looked at her with sheer disappointment and something else I rarely saw in him: hurt. They didn't speak for the remainder of the day.

I visited my father almost every day once he was home. A part of me was resentful because I didn't have time for me, because I couldn't be happy and experience the array of emotions and feelings I always envisioned I'd have as an expectant mother. I kept thinking, *Dammit. I can't even have my baby in peace. I can't even rejoice in that wonder of life.*

The majority of my time was spent thinking about Pop and making the hour run from my home to his house in Beverly Hills. And, yes, I felt crummy that I even allowed myself the luxury of feeling so self-involved.

How could I be so selfish, so uncaring? My father was dying. My father was in pain and all I cared about was having some attention focused on me. But the anger did not pass gently into acceptance; instead, it stormed into rage.

I was furious with everything and everybody, and I was mad as hell with God. What a cruel hoax: I had never really known my father and had spent much of my young life treating him rudely while he ignored me. Now when we finally make peace with each other and finally become close, *boom*, he gets cancer.

I was furious with my father for smoking cigarettes and I was ready to take on every major tobacco company. I was pissed at his choice to have radiation instead of surgery, and I was even mad that he got throat cancer instead of a different type—something more easily cured.

In the weeks, months and years to come, I played upon that anger like a missionary. I didn't treat people badly, I just didn't allow anyone to be close to me. I still don't have many friends.

About the only people I allowed near me at that time were Guy, my mother and my father. My love for Dad was still blossoming and his feelings for me were just as embryonic.

When I visited him, I talked a lot about my unborn baby. We knew it was a boy and he seemed to delight in my ever-growing stomach.

"You're getting uglier every day, Trace Face," he'd wink. I'd laugh. Before his illness, I used to tease him about changing diapers and baby-sitting and, amazingly, he was really looking forward to it. I guess age and the problems he and I had had as father and daughter mellowed him in a way and made him feel more secure about caring for a child.

But conversation became harder and harder. Since he had to cover a hole in a tube which helped him to breathe, he didn't speak very much. He hated to do it, but he hated writing even more. The tube in his throat gave him an excuse for not talking to someone if he didn't want to. Everyone wanted to see Sammy Davis Jr. when he was sick, but Dad only wanted to see the people he truly loved and respected.

Frank Sinatra was ripped apart that Dad was dying.

He was just a mess; I'll never forget it. I had never seen Frank so bent out of shape, ever, in my entire life. He and Dad were the best of friends and their lives had been entwined for decades—all the stuff they'd been through together, the highs and lows of their careers, and now Sammy was checking out.

I remember how a few months earlier, when Dad was in remission, he'd joked about leaving Frank: "I'm dying," he said lightly. "Frank's going to do another 15 years on stage because I'm dying—you realize that, don't you? Frank is never going to die." Dad laughed at his private joke about how his shenanigans used to age his big brother, Frank.

Frank was a lot older than Dad and had plenty more problems but never cancer. Frank called him "the Kid." He also called him Charlie and Sam—the only person who ever did because my grandfather was Sam; Pop was always Sammy. Rat Pack aside, these two guys truly loved each other, the love one man has for a brother or a friend who is closer than life.

So Frank would come over to the house and spend a few minutes with Dad. He always looked pretty grim when he climbed the stairs to Dad's bedroom. He was a different man when he emerged later: fallen, stunned, head bowed, jaw set. He wouldn't look at anyone, just fade through the glass doors to the circular driveway and pace around in a sobbing daze. I wanted so to comfort him, but held back a little, respecting his privacy. Frank didn't want me or anyone else to see him crying.

In the midst of all the strife with Dad, we suffered yet another blow. Our close friend, Richard Toufankian, was killed in a freak accident. His wife, Madeleine, was an old friend of mine, and she had just sent out the invitations for his 30th birthday party. Richard and Maddy were the golden couple. They had been together years but married only less than a year, and so very much in love.

Richard had been rear-ended on the freeway. A minor

traffic accident, but he couldn't drive the car. So he'd called Maddy and she'd driven over to pick him up. When she pulled up, he said he would drive and walked in front of the car to talk to the tow truck driver. A car in the fast lane hit something and cut across all four lanes, smashing into Richard. The impact lifted Richard into the air and smashed him head first into the back of the tow truck. He died in Maddy's arms on the side of the freeway. I went to see Maddy as soon as I got the news. She opened the door and asked me, "What am I going to do, Tracey?" I truly was stunned. I had no answers to give her, only my love, my friendship, my support. All I could do was hug her and be there.

It was hard accepting Richard's death. He was a wonderful person and also close to my age. And his death came when someone else so close to me was dying. It was almost too much to bear.

I didn't tell Dad about Richard. I wanted only to give him happy, good tidings. Guy and I had been saving the news that we wanted to name our baby Sam, after Dad. We were waiting for the birth to let him know. But now the doctors said my father probably wouldn't live another month, so we decided to tell Pop right away. We both sat with him in his bedroom. Guy loved Dad as much as I did and was so excited and happy about the news.

"Dad, we have something to tell you," I said. I was starting to choke up, so Guy had to finish.

"Mr. D," he said, "we decided to name our baby Sam, after you."

My father said nothing for a moment. He just trembled and then he started to cry. "Thanks for my gift," he whispered.

Guy and I went back downstairs in tears, and Dad's doctor took me outside to talk.

"Look," he said, "your father will not be alive when your baby is born. He will be dead. I don't want you to hold out any false hope. He will not be alive."

He was just trying to prepare me, but his words stung.

I thought him heartless, insensitive, a real bastard. Later, though, I would thank him for his frankness.

I went back inside the house and up to Dad's room. Altovise had joined him. His window was open and I knew he had heard what the doctor said. He looked me in the eye and said, "I'm not going anywhere until I see my grandson. I'm just staying around to see Sam. After that, I've got nothing to live for."

Little things we'd always taken for granted suddenly had a profound sense of urgency while my father was ill. Sitting outside just listening to the wind and the birds became a religious experience; inhaling the pungent eucalyptus from the trees dotting the lawn was a sacrament. Dad loved to go outside and just sit and drink in the air.

Four French doors from the living room opened to the emerald garden of my father's sanctuary. At first, he and I would walk from the bedroom to the living room. Later, he had to use the wheelchair. He hated it. But he always brightened when he went into the living room because it was full of happy memories. It was the place where Dad enjoyed his friends, and it was where Guy and I had exchanged our wedding vows. The room had a long, brownish bar, where Dad had loved to hold court whenever he entertained. I think he was a frustrated bartender in a previous life. A large glass coffee table held letters from Jack Benny and one of Judy Garland's ruby slippers from *The Wizard of Oz*, sealed in a special case. It had been a gift from Liza Minnelli. Dad also kept his Kennedy Center honor and some old belt buckles on the table.

The living room overlooked a lawn that swept all the way to the back fence, which was lined with eucalyptus trees. A giant replica of a *Planet of the Apes* gorilla stood sentry in the pool area. It had been a gift for the man who had everything. Dad had about two-and-a-half acres, with a swimming pool and pool house. He'd added his "kitchen," which doubled as a guest house.

Pop liked to linger a bit in the living room during our journeys to the patio. It was as though he were trying to remember something or preserve a picture in his mind. Once outside, we didn't do very much except feel the air stir around us and watch the birds hop from tree to tree. Every now and then, one of the security guys would pass through with a shotgun on his shoulder, a reminder that my father wasn't just any father. Dad never seemed to notice the security—to him it was on the same level as a leaf blowing by or a fly buzzing about. He would just sit there and not say anything.

Sometimes, he and I would hold hands in silence. Dad was trying to be so brave. I knew he was scared, but he didn't want me to know. We would go for what seemed an eternity without speaking—you know that you're really close to someone when you can do that. At last, my father and I were close.

We used to joke a lot about how close we'd become in so short a time. Pop and Guy also were very close, and we'd joke about that, too.

"Do you love Guy more than me?" I would ask my father. And he'd smile in that deliciously wicked little way of his and say, "Yeah. Sometimes."

But as the baby's due date approached, it became increasingly more difficult for me to drive to see Dad. I was ripe, uncomfortable and cranky. Worst of all, I had to go to the bathroom every few minutes. The pressure on my bladder was tremendous. The baby's due date came and went. I was 10 days late. But my father was still alive. I was doing all sorts of things to bring on the birth: My mom and I took long walks; I jumped up and down, I ate weird salads—anything to start labor.

Part of me wanted Sam to arrive so Dad could see him before he died. But another part of me knew that when Sam came, Dad would stop living. Sheer will kept my father alive, but I was beginning to panic—I kept thinking he'd die before the baby was born. I was going to my doctor every day; on the 10th day I threatened to kill him if he didn't take out the baby. Hell hath no fury like a crazy pregnant woman. He took one look at me, did an ultrasound and announced it was showtime.

I couldn't believe it finally was happening; I just prayed that Dad would hold on, and mentally called to him not to die. My father had been so prepared to be a grandfather. He was excited about that chapter of life, helping to raise little Sam and doing things with him that he had neglected doing with me, Mark and Jeff. I know he would have been a good granddad. I even had fantasies of dropping Sam off at Pop's house so they could play together while I went shopping or to work; I dreamed of sitting backstage at one of Dad's shows and taking Sam, dressed smartly in a little suit and looking like a little man, the way his grandfather had when he was young. No, hang in there, Pop. Your grandson's on the way.

I called Guy at work. "Go home. Get my bag. I'm checking in this instant."

Guy was freaking. "OK. OK. You sure? OK. OK. Where are you? Do you want me to come get you?"

"No, Guy. I'm already at the hospital. You come to me in Tarzana."

"OK. OK." He hung up.

When he arrived, I was already hooked up to monitors and my doctor had started to induce labor. But I wouldn't dilate; I was having really strong contractions, but nothing happened. Finally, after a day and a half, my doctor said they would do a cesarean section, which was fine by me. I was terrified of having a vaginal delivery—just the thought of a baby coming that way. My girlfriends and I always said it's like pushing a softball through a button-hole. A nurse sat me up, leaned me forward and gave me an epidural anesthetic in my back to block the pain.

Sam was born April 20, 1990, with a tangle of jet-black hair crawling down his neck. He was just gorgeous, a little sleeping rugrat. Guy cried when he was born and cried every day for three days every time he looked at his son.

My tears were sweet, with the joy of my son's birth and the knowledge that his grandfather would see him. I fell asleep happy for the first time in months. When I woke up, they brought Sam, wrapped tightly in a little blanket. He was just lying there, sleeping. So pretty, so pure. He didn't cry.

We went home after two days in the hospital, but I didn't stay. We just dumped everything off, I sat for about 30 minutes to gain a little strength and then we were off to see Dad. The pressure from Shirley to get to Dad's without delay was enormous. There was no real time for me, and no real time for joy. I could barely walk, almost bent in two, but I was determined to have my father meet his grandson. I thought the baby would be a good tonic for him.

That was such a wonderful day, a day touched by goodness and the whisper of new life. Dad was sitting in a huge, oversized chair in his bedroom. His brown skin almost blended with the rich, milk chocolate brown velour of the chair. He wore a robe and pajama bottoms. He had a tracheotomy tube in his throat and an IV in his arm. His neck was bandaged where the tumor was. Funny, it hadn't been so noticeable in the beginning, almost as if you could just slice it off and everything would be fine.

I waddled in, spiked with pain. I bit my tongue to force myself to put on a happy face, to hide my agony from Pop. I prayed he wouldn't notice how bad I was wobbling. Guy had his arm around me and Sam; his touch helped ease the sting and propel me across the room to my father.

Now, Dad didn't really have baby smarts. He hadn't held many tots over the years, and I was a little anxious.

I eased Sam onto his lap and started to adjust the baby so they'd both be comfortable. "Pop, make sure you support his little neck and…." He cut me off and gave me that Jack Benny look of total indignation, a look that always got laughs in every club he played.

It was hard for Dad to speak, but he did. "Trace, dear, whose daughter are you?" he whispered. "I think I may have held you once or twice."

"Oh, Pop. I know," I whined with a smile.

I pulled away my hand and left Sam in Dad's lap.

"Guy. Look. Look," I squealed, after I sat down. "Look at that strong family line." My son was truly Sammy Davis Jr.'s grandchild: Sam looked like Dad, only his skin was light. Both the similarity and contrast were stunning.

My father smiled at the tiny creature in his lap and tears slid down his cheeks. For his part, Sam, new to life, just opened his eyes, blinked and stared in that all-knowing way babies have. He didn't cry a peep. I sat there and kept thinking, *Please, Sam, don't cry. Please don't get Pop upset.* But my baby was quiet, almost as if he knew that this was a historic moment.

Dad was worn out from speaking but he managed to squeeze out a few more words. "He's beautiful, Trace. I love you, baby," he said. He leaned over and delicately kissed Sam on the cheek.

Alto came up the stairs and into the bedroom, and the mood was broken. She began buzzing around trying to be helpful, rearranging Dad's pillows and fussing with his legs on the ottoman. Dad slapped her hand away and she left, only to return moments later with a camera to take pictures of Pop with his grandchild.

I noticed Guy frowning while all this was going on. He leaned into Dad and said, "Mr. D, do you want any pictures?"

"No," he snapped.

Altovise persisted and tried to talk Dad into it, but she only succeeded in making him mad.

"Dammit. How the hell can you get the film developed without the tabloids knowing?" Dad didn't want any remembrances that showed him the way he now looked.

Talking finally strained Pop's throat and he broke into a coughing fit. He handed Sam to Guy and got back into bed. But we were all so happy. In one sweet brush stroke of time, Sammy and Sam had braided their lives. I forgot my pain.

Liza Minnelli showed up one day and sat for an hour or so in the sitting room with me, Guy and Sam. Liza was so frightened. She kept biting her lip, the way a 10-year-old does when she doesn't want to face some difficult situation. Being a witness to Dad's dying was very hard for Liza, just as it was for everyone else who deeply cared for him. She reached over and held our hands, and her eyes began to water.

"I haven't done anything like this since Mama died," she said, chewing her lip and squeezing our hands even tighter. "I don't know if I'm strong enough to go upstairs without falling apart."

"Oh, Liza. It's just great that you're here. Don't worry about anything else. It's really just OK," I said. "You know Pop—just the fact that you came will make him feel good. He'll understand if you can't handle seeing him, because he knows he doesn't look great. And Liza, Dad doesn't want his friends to remember him that way. God, that's killing him as much as the cancer."

Liza nodded and smiled a thin smile. Then she fired off questions as if she were preparing for a show. She wanted to know everything, every detail, because she wanted to be strong for Dad. She asked me how bad the cancer was and what he looked like. She swallowed hard as I told her, and I felt my throat turn to sandpaper as I forced out the words.

"He's real tiny, Liza, smaller than you've ever seen him." She kept her eyes fixed on mine and chewed her lip some more. "The tumor looks like a softball is stuck under the skin on his neck, and, and"—I had trouble saying this, but I knew she wanted to hear everything—"it gives off a horrible odor. Nauseating. Cancer stinks."

We both fought back tears.

"Will he recognize me?" she asked. I didn't answer.

Liza held the baby for a little while, nuzzling his neck and playing with his little fingers as he slept. Then Guy walked her up the five or six steps to Dad's bedroom. He stayed with her until she turned and nodded that she was OK, that she could handle being alone with Pop.

Liza stayed upstairs in the bedroom with Dad for about an hour. When she came down, she looked at us and we looked at her. There was nothing to say.

I went to see my father just about every day. We didn't talk much but he always focused on me and Sam and smiled. Then one day, he had changed. Apparently, the night before, his tube had clogged and he'd been without air for a short period of time, enough for him to suffer brain damage. I could see in his eyes that he wasn't the same. He had this look on his face that said, "I'm not all here." That's when Dad really stopped trying to talk. After that I just held his hand and watched the tumor leak its poison.

One hand was like marble, cold, smooth and lifeless. Death is a cold place, I mused, shaking off a chill. His other hand was feverishly hot from the cancer. He woke up a little bit, saw me and said, "I love you, Trace Face." Those were the last words my father ever spoke to me.

Two days later, he slipped into a coma. He was consumed by pain and there was no chance he'd recover.

Late one night, I couldn't sleep so I turned on the television and caught a show with a psychologist named David Viscott. He was talking to someone who was losing a loved one to AIDS. The process had consumed this person. Viscott's advice was to abandon hope when it is realistic to do so. That way, you are better able to handle the later stages of a terminal illness. His words clung to me, and I considered his advice.

But I continued my visits.

On one visit I remember looking at my father through a kaleidoscope of tears. He seemed so small and fragile, lost amid a tangle of sheets and tubes. He slept an uneasy, uncertain slumber.

He was curled in an attempt at fetal comfort as he slept, his delicate body forming but a tiny valley in the bed. The hospital bed seemed so clinical, so clunky, so out of place in that room, a room that once held so much laughter and life.

I sat in a chair by his bed, listening to the machinery of death and wanting to shut it down. I shifted my gaze from Dad, and allowed my eyes to stray around the pale yellow-and-white bedroom. Two buckets jammed with a thousand yellow roses from Bill Cosby added a little warmth and a lovely link to life. Too bad Dad couldn't see what his dear old friend had sent. I closed my eyes and remembered the dinners I'd had with Dad and Bill. Memories have a way of comforting.

I kept my eyes closed and tunneled deep within myself, stretching every fiber I had to somehow spiritually touch my father. I squeezed my eyes shut harder. Maybe there was some of that Sammy Davis Jr. energy left—that spunk, that spirited high that rubbed off on everyone around him. Maybe I could grab some and lock it in my soul.

The room was all so wrong. All of Dad's things were still there, and he was still there, but his spirit was slowly moving on to another place.

I unlocked my eyes and scanned the now-silent wall of televisions—one for entertainment, four for security. I swept past the miles of books that ran from floor to ceiling. *The Joy of Cooking. The Joy of Sex.* The joy of Sammy Davis Jr., who loved to read. Suddenly I was drawn to every object in the room, as if some gentle force were ushering me about, a tour guide of the artifacts of my father's life. I ran my hand over the books and grazed the glass of his tropical fish tank. I opened the drawer in the table by his bed and saw the gun he kept there. Like father, like son, I thought, remembering how my grandfather always slept with a shotgun under his bed.

My foot nudged the Louis Vuitton satchel Dad always kept near him. Without looking, I knew it held a great deal of money. Dad always had enormous amounts of cash; he was a professional spender. He threw money around like confetti, and every freeloader flocked to him. To say he was generous is an understatement: Dad was the missing link in the philanthropic chain. He gave street beggars hundred dollar bills and stuffed more fifties into the sweaty palms of bellboys and coat-check people than I'd like to remember. He also quietly helped out old friends who needed surgery, or who lost jobs or homes, or were just going through a bad time. He never asked for anything in return.

His excesses shadowed me as I wandered into the bathroom. Dad had practically every shampoo and soap ever made, all piled high on decorative trays on the Lucite counter. And he damn near had a different toothbrush for each tooth: natural bristles and checkered stems, narrow brushes, wide ones. I inherited that particular brand of lunacy from Pop—I always loved using different soaps, sponges and shampoos.

Dad was a goof. I used to tell him he didn't need to have an indoor swimming pool because you could do the backstroke in his tub. It had gold faucets and a little Romanesque statue of a boy who peed into the bathtub at the push of a button. That always cracked me up, and I remember how Dad would drag people in there to watch the golden boy in action.

I picked up a small bar of sea kelp soap and inhaled its breezy sweetness before swapping it for a whiff of Aramis cologne. My head filled with the fragrance of my father. The aroma I had known all my life stayed with me as I left the bathroom and drifted back to Dad's sickbed.

He rustled the sheets a bit in his sleep and shivered. I pulled the white cotton blanket a little higher over his shoulder and let my hand linger for a while on his arm. I needed to somehow silently tell him I was there and that I loved him. The words rang somewhere in my head, as conversations with yourself have a way of doing. I pushed once again with my mind, trying to contact him with my thoughts. But there was no response, just the eerie, sad rasping of a dying man. He was as frail as my infant son and just as vulnerable, and that terrified me.

Light from the afternoon sun danced across the fish tank on the other side of the bed and achieved a perfect marriage with the pale yellow walls. I always thought my father looked lost in that enormous room. But it was so...Sammy Davis Jr.

Then I bent over and kissed his forehead and left him for another day.

Sometimes, while driving the 40 miles from our home to Dad's place in Beverly Hills, I'd stare out the window at the rushing asphalt and imagine it was all a bad dream, that I'd wake up and Pop would be laughing and joking, making plans for a new concert, playing with his grandson.

It was, of course, no dream. It was real and reality sucks. The best we could do was to make every second count and just be near him.

When the nurse changed Dad's bed, it was Guy who held my father while the bed was remade with fresh linens. My husband loved Pop as if he were his own father. One day, I watched Guy help the nurse change Dad's bed. He gently slipped his hands under my father and scooped him into his arms, as you would a sleeping child. Guy cradled him, delicately placing Dad's head in the crook of his arm. Guy was so tender, but Dad nonetheless winced with pain. His body was like an eggshell; there was nothing to cushion the assault. By this time, Dad had wasted to about 70 pounds or so. Pop used to call his "fighting weight" about 120. Now he was like a stick-figure drawing of himself.

It was then I wished my father was dead.

He was in agony; pain was ripping him apart and I wanted the hurt to stop. I began to feel his pain, and the sadness of his suffering stabbed my soul. I could not bear to watch his jaw tighten or his eyes squeeze to slits as he fought the searing agony. I prayed for his death, and I prayed to God to forgive me.

I began to talk to him: "Pop, if you want to die, I understand. You can just let go and I'll be all right and make sure everybody else is all right. You can let go. You'll always be with us. You're a part of me and you're a part of Sam, and I'll always be a part of you. It's all right," I whispered.

Murphy came down to have the talk I knew was coming. He was a direct sort of man, soft-spoken and always very respectful toward Dad. He had been with Pop since the old days, the vaudeville circuit of the Will Mastin Trio. He loved my father with a passion, and always looked up to him. Now, he spoke quietly and without hesitation.

"Tracey, your father left instructions that you are to be the one who makes the decision."

For a second, I had no idea what he meant. "The decision?" I muttered.

"Yes. He wants you to decide when it's time to pull the plug."

"What about Alto? What about you?" My voice came out as a pathetic squeak. But my rational side knew it had to be this way.

Murphy gave me a kindly look. "I can't," he said simply. "I don't want that to be my last memory of Sammy. I'm too old, honey." Murphy consulted with me for a while and I agreed to be the one.

The doctors told us they could give Dad more morphine to ease the pain but it would hasten his death. I looked at everyone: Murphy, Guy, Shirley, Alto. They were all hurting in their separate ways. Then I went back to see Dad. His face was creased in agony, one lonely tear cruising down his cheek.

I returned to the doctors. "Do it," I said.

Chapter Seventeen

May 16, 1990. The phone rang at 5:56 in the morning.

"He's dead, isn't he?"

"Yeah, he died about five minutes ago." It was my brother Mark.

I thought the past year had drained my tear ducts, but my body found a way to manufacture more, and thimblefuls fell from my eyes to Guy's shoulder. I cried until my eyelids grew tender and swollen. Guy rubbed my shoulder and let me be.

My mother had come to stay with us when Sam was born and hadn't yet gone home. She had heard the phone ring, heard my sobs and was now in the doorway. She nodded and said, "Was that...?"

"Yes," I said.

She started crying herself, leaning against a wall.

No matter what anyone says, you're never really prepared for death. I thought knowing it would happen to Dad would make it easier when the time came. Bullshit. It was horrible watching him inch toward death and it was terrible when it was over.

We all knew his death was for the best. Dad was at peace. It was over: the pain, the anxiety, the humiliation of a terminal illness. You have no idea what this did to my father, a proud man who valued dignity.

Dad knew he was slipping fast, but he certainly didn't want to be forgotten. Weeks before his death, he told me not to let Sammy Davis Jr.—what he was, what he stood for and what he had accomplished—die with him.

"You know, it's up to you," he said one day. "Like my father always used to say, 'You're the onliest Davis!' It's up to you, Tracey, to keep me going and I'm asking you to do that— to seek out who my real friends are, find out who you can trust and who you can't trust and just keep me alive. When I go, I want people to be crying their fucking eyes out. I want them to be bent over just sobbing, then go on," he said.

They were.

Dad's death was a front-page story around the world, and the lead on every TV and radio newscast. The Las Vegas strip went dark for 10 minutes in his honor. That really blew my mind, because the only other times Las Vegas did that were for the assassinations of John F. Kennedy and Martin Luther King Jr., and briefly for Dean Martin. Through my grief, I was proud of my father, proud he was so great that his death became an international event; proud that he was much beloved. It was a blessing that I didn't have to call people to let them know he was dead, and have to recount the whole story over and over again. The phone rang incessantly, and my house became choked with flowers and baskets of fruit.

Madeleine was in Amsterdam, still getting over Richard's death, and she called me two hours after Dad had died.

"It's all over the news, Tracey," she said. "Are you all right? Do you need me to fly home?"

I told her no. I knew Madeleine didn't want to be home and didn't want to be in her house. I wouldn't have been able to do it, and I didn't expect her to. There was no way she could handle another death so soon after Richard's, but I loved her for wanting to be there for me.

Madeleine, like so many other people in the world, learned of Dad's death on television. The media had been camped outside my father's home for weeks, so reporters were primed to file their bulletins. Paparazzi had even tried to jump the fence to get a peek at Pop, and every time a car pulled up to the gate, they pounced on it like a bunch of vultures to see what celebrity they could fill their lenses with. When I pulled into the driveway the day my father died, I hardly noticed them.

Shirley and Murphy were doing a wonderful job of seeing to the tedious details of the funeral, but I passed on a few of my father's wishes just the same. He didn't want an open casket and all he wanted on his headstone was: THE ENTERTAINER. They understood. I'm not too sure Altovise did. Shirley told me it was too late for the headstone engraving. Alto apparently disregarded Dad's wishes and had her own version in mind. So my father's tombstone has a small story on it: his name; date of birth; date of death; and THE ENTERTAINER; HE DID IT ALL; YOUR LOVING WIFE ALTOVISE, FATHER OF TRACEY, MARK, JEFF AND MANNY."

Manny? That kid she wanted to adopt and Dad didn't? We had barely seen him, including Pop. He wasn't even there when Dad was dying. I feel sorry for Manny because he was put into a no-win situation. Shirley and everyone else told Alto not to junk up Dad's headstone that way. But she was his wife.

And that was the least of what Alto did. The night before Dad's funeral, she held a wake at the funeral home. I told Shirley I wouldn't be there. Why, so I could look at a box holding my father? There was no way I could deal with that, and I knew Dad would understand.

Guy went because he thought one of us should be there. He returned home with an odd look on his face. It was part despair, part disgust.

"The casket was open, Trace," he said.

"What?"

"Worst part is, it didn't look like him. They tried to puff up his face on one side so it would be even with the side that had the tumor," Guy said.

"Shit," I replied.

"Your dad's face was so chiseled and thin. They made him look freakish, strange. It wasn't his face—it was too...plump. And, Trace, there was a photographer there."

"What do you mean? Some dude hanging out?"

"Well, no. He was inside the funeral home taking pictures," Guy said.

"You're kidding me? Pop wouldn't want anything like that," I said. "Who the hell allowed that?"

"It gets worse," Guy said. "He took some pictures of your Dad in the coffin."

I was like a cannonball hurling through the barrel—hot, smoking and lethal. I called Shirley. She wasn't home, but the next day we arrived early for the funeral procession, and I grabbed her and told her what had happened. She, too, was appalled. We had to act fast to get that film before it turned up in supermarket tabloids.

So Shirley asked David Steinberg if he could find out about the photographer. David fibbed and told the photographer that Frank was so angry about the pictures that he'd have him killed if he didn't turn them over. This wasn't true, of course, but it shook up the photographer and he surrendered the film. That's when I spotted the guy and ran over to him. He probably thought I was the hit woman because that's how enraged I was.

"Why were you taking pictures of my father in a casket?" I screamed at him.

"Because Altovise asked me to," he said.

I just stood there with my mouth open. I had no idea who he worked for, but I knew beyond a shadow of a doubt that if he had kept the film, those pictures would have ended up in a tabloid.

My father's funeral was like a presidential motorcade. Thousands of people stood on the roadways from Dad's house to Forest Lawn Memorial Park, taking off their hats as the hearse went by, clapping and shouting, "Sammy, we love you." Guy and I looked at each other, awed that total strangers would leave their homes to pay tribute to my dad. The limo moved very slowly, allowing us to see each thoughtful face. I remember one fan had shaved words into his hair: LUV YOU SAMMY. Guy and I were both warmed by their embrace. Everyone said my father's funeral would be a private affair. It wasn't. Legions of celebrities turned out, and his fans were just as much a part of it. They all loved him, too. Maybe not like my mother or myself, but they did love him. It was a beautiful tribute—the more love the better. So many fans showed up at Forest Lawn that they had to be moved through the cemetery in shifts.

I don't remember much about the actual service. Some things are best a blur, and the funeral of someone you hold dear definitely falls into that category. I do remember it was a blazingly hot day. God was truly smiling on Pop because he loved heat so much! I remember Jesse Jackson called Dad "Mr. Bojangles" and said he's earned the right to rest now. Then he asked everyone to stand as a recording of Sammy Davis Jr. singing "Mr. Bojangles" was played. I sobbed uncontrollably, as I always had whenever Dad sang that song. It brought me back to Las Vegas: "I love you, but I've never really liked you...."

Rabbi Allen Freehling momentarily shook the wisps of memory from me when he went to the microphone and talked about how Dad had fought the good fight against cancer and finally had gone "gently into the good night."

I remember how Frank rubbed my back as we were walking out—he had canceled a sold-out concert at Radio City Music Hall in New York to be there for Dad. And I certainly remember Berry Gordy shoving past me so he could have a better view of the burial. Guy had to restrain himself from belting the Motown maestro. Instead, he put his hand on Berry's shoulder and firmly said, "This is his daughter, man." Berry just looked and said, "Oh." He quickly moved out of the way and let us through. We walked toward the front and passed Tony Danza, sobbing uncontrollably. Pop had been crazy about Tony and now I saw just how crazy Tony had been for my father. Shirley MacLaine had a tortured look on her face and she touched me with a warm smile.

When the service was over, I went to Dad's bronze casket. It looked so stately surrounded by flowers, ferns and ficus. I thought how happy he'd be that his final curtain was a class act. "I've Got to Be Me" had played during the service, and that had been Pop. Even in death, he got to do things in his own style. Then I bent over and kissed the coffin. I had said goodbye so many times. This was the last. I had wanted to hold on to the moment, to linger with my father, but I felt I couldn't. The TV cameras were on me and all the people were looking. I felt so rushed.

It was only fitting that my father was buried in a family plot next to his dad, Sammy Davis Sr., in a walled courtyard high atop a hill called the Garden of Honors. His grandmother Peewee and Will Mastin also lie in nearby plots. On the other side of the garden is the grave of Sam Cooke.

The drive back to Dad's house was a blur. When we arrived, I was saved from emotional drowning by Billy Crystal and my baby. An old friend of mine, Leslie Johnson, stayed with Sam at Dad's house while we went to the funeral. Which meant she wasn't able to attend, but she was the type of friend who would give you the proverbial shirt off her back.

Sam was like a little magnet: Everyone wanted to hold him, touch him, hug him. He so much resembled my father, despite the pale skin and hair that had considerably lightened since his birth. Then I heard a voice making its way across the room.

"Excuse me. Excuse me. Thank you. OK. Give him up! Give him up!" It was Billy, whose impersonation of Pop was more Sammy Davis Jr. than Dad himself. Billy plopped a diaper on his shoulder and I surrendered my son. He walked around the reception with Sam for two hours. And it was just as it was when I brought my baby to meet Dad that first time—not a peep. He just slept on Billy's shoulder. He was a real pro, a father who joyously shared the raising of his children with his wife.

Billy and all of Dad's other friends were so wonderful to us. Bill Cosby called me and told me if I ever needed him for anything, he was merely a telephone call away. And he meant it.

Shirley worked tirelessly to ensure that Pop had a proper send-off. She organized the funeral reception, and used the same caterer Dad always used for his parties. There was plenty to eat, plenty to drink and lots of music. Pop got his wish: Everyone cried, then the party began.

Chapter Eighteen

The night was dark and thin, like a shadow world—an appropriate world for me after my father's death. I was there, but not there; a silhouette rather than reality. At the same time, I felt edgy, prickly and very afraid.

It was so hard to think of my father as dead. And no one would let me forget. His name was still all over the radio, and every newsstand we passed carried big headlines about the funeral. Wherever I turned, I saw Dad's face. In a way, it was comforting, because I didn't want to let go of him, and any reminder was welcome. But in another way, I felt as if I had been dropped into a Cuisinart.

I barely spoke to Guy on the drive back to Simi Valley, and he had few words for me. We were drained and felt the void left by Dad's death. I was bone tired; I envied Sam, who continued to sleep peacefully in his car bed. I glanced at my son through the rearview mirror and something stirred in me, some sort of primal desire to be an infant once again, protected and secure…with two parents.

I couldn't seem to shake the profound unease nibbling at my soul that something could happen to Mom. If I had been able to, I would have read the steady darkening of Guy's mood and realized the hammering tension between us. By the time we pulled into our driveway, the fear that my mother would also die had consumed me.

"I'm going to stay with Mom tonight," I announced to Guy. "I just want to change my clothes and put Sam to bed."

He stood there with his hands outstretched and his mouth open. "Going to your mother's house? Tonight? What do you mean?"

"I need her right now." I thought Guy would understand. I didn't think I'd have to explain.

"What about me? Don't you need me? What are you doing?"

"Dammit, Guy, don't you get it? My dad is dead! Mom's all I've got. I'm afraid, you pinhead! I'm afraid something will happen to her, too, and I won't have any parents at all. I just want to be with her. Please understand."

Guy was furious. He was hurting as much as I was, but we couldn't seem to merge our mutual pain or soothe each other. Instead, I dealt only with my own misery and left him for the night to be with my mother. All the way to Mom's house, I thought of Dad. My mind unspooled the happy highlights of the past few years, the years Dad and I were fortunate to have together after we both learned forgiveness. If my father and I could figure things out, couldn't my husband and I?

When I returned home, Guy was ready to explode. So was I. A simmering feud set in. We had been together so long, ever since we both were kids, really. We were more like two friends than husband and wife.

Guy and I had been through a lot with Pop, the baby, my auto accident and Richard's death; plus Guy was having a tough go of it as an actor. We both had hit bottom and seemed to be stepping on each other to get back up. With postpartum blues, mourning and paranoia coloring all reason, I didn't know how to throw my husband a lifeline. He had been glued to my side through everything, and my father's illness and death had terribly affected him. Guy loved Dad as much as he loved his own father.

His parents had divorced when he was seven years old. His mother remarried and Guy was raised by his stepfather, Ted Garner, whose name Guy embraced. Guy was born Guido Aldo DaRe; his uncle was Aldo Ray, a gruff-voiced actor who was a big star in the 1950s and 1960s, and a friend of my parents before he died from alcoholism. He was a natural at acting.

So Guy was a DaRe and then a Garner and, when he married me, he became a Davis. I know how much I disliked being known as Tracey Two Commas, so I know Guy would have preferred his own identity as well. Part of my depression was indeed that I no longer was Sammy's Kid, I no longer had my father. But Guy's depression probably had been building ever since his older sister, Taryn, had died from complications of lupus a year before we were married. The tortured months of Dad's decline certainly carved some more ugly notches on Guy's spirit as well.

And there I was, a poster child for postpartum blues.

Put another way, Guy and I were like two clumps of plastique waiting to explode. All we needed was a detonator.

We found it a short time later when Guy went off to Israel to star in the movie *An American Citizen*. This was Guy's big chance, not only to break into movies, but also to slough off the decaying skin of what was slowly becoming a bad marriage.

He jumped for joy; I dug deeper into a self-indulgent funk.

I called Guy twice a day during the seven weeks he was in the Middle East. Big mistake. My calls always came at the wrong moment and we'd end up fighting. It was the first time since we had been together that we'd been separated for an extended period of time. It also was the first time he got recognized on the streets. *An American Citizen* was big in Israel; Guy was doing an excellent job, and was honored for what he had done—on his own, without my name or my father's name. Guy enjoyed the freedom he had thousands of miles away. Who could blame him?

Mother's Day—my first one—and the anniversary of Dad's death arrived around the same time. Guy didn't call. Nor did he send flowers. Suddenly, it was my fifth birthday party all over again, and I was home with Mom waiting for Dad to show up. I promised myself I wouldn't cry.

After the shoot Guy returned to Hollywood, where no

one recognized him, and to a crappy marriage and a seriously needy wife he couldn't handle. I tried to get him to talk about our problems, but he wouldn't. I knew that prying words out of Guy was like opening a stubborn clam. He was a very closed man at that time, a lot like Dad in that regard. He never wanted to know why: Just show him the big picture. So I guess it's true that we really do seek men in our father's image.

There had been so many disruptions in my life, so many losses and separations. My parents' divorce loomed somewhere in my mind, and I remembered Mom saying when I was growing up, "You don't stay in a crappy environment—it's not worth it." But she talked with me about divorce around the time Dad was dying and admitted that she would have stuck it out longer with Pop if she had been a little older and a little wiser. "When I look at the problems we were having, they don't seem so bad now, they're not insurmountable," Mom told me. And, so, I clung to my marriage.

Guy and I continued to snipe at each other. He wanted change and didn't know how to tell me, nor did he know how to achieve it. I wanted attention, and all the rage I grew up having against my father for ignoring me as a child now resurfaced and was focused on Guy.

About a month after Guy's return from Israel, I turned 30, and Guy announced he no longer wanted to be married. A friend suggested we see a marriage counselor. I was all for it. Guy, though, would have preferred root canal to counseling. Still, I went ahead and made an appointment.

It's so hard to sit down and try not only to tell a complete stranger what's wrong with your relationship, but also to unleash deeply personal emotional issues. Where in the world do you start? So I began by talking about the most inconsequential stuff, and Guy talked about how much he loved being in Israel. He said he loved Sam but didn't know how to live with me anymore because he needed some breathing room and I refused to give him any. That took care of the hour. We never went back. By the time we got home,

Guy was trying to figure out where he was going to live.

I was bereft. I begged him not to leave, but that only led to more arguments. Guy went to a hotel for a few days. He wanted to come home every night so he could help put Sam to bed. I decided to take the high road and not use Sam as a weapon, so I allowed Guy to do it.

One of those nights, we got into the worst fight we'd ever had, and Guy told me he no longer loved me. He didn't want to be married, he said, and he was leaving for good. I became hysterical and sobbed uncontrollably. Guy thundered out the door and left.

The next morning I blasted off the bed, grabbed a suitcase, packed a few things, kissed Sam and told the nanny I would be in Tahoe with my mother. I didn't see the concern on the nanny's face when she saw me, weeping and wrecked, get into my car. She was terrified.

Once I started driving, I thought I'd begin to feel better and that everything would work out—I'd call Guy and he'd be home, upset and wanting me back. I had been gone for less than 10 minutes when I made the first call. He wasn't there. I called every 10 minutes until I got him on the phone.

"Guy, please—can't we get back together? Please?" I knew he heard the panic in my voice.

He waited a beat before saying simply, "No."

"Can't you see I'm falling apart, Guy? Can't you tell what a wreck I am? I can't believe you want to end our marriage right now. My God, Dad's dead! And we have Sam! How can you do this to me?"

He didn't answer at first. Then he told me he didn't want to talk to me, and hung up. Maybe I should have called a friend, like Julie or Diane or Maddy. But, at that moment, I didn't care what they had to say because I had decided that no one really cared about me or what happened to me. I only wanted to hear kind words from one person: Guy. I was reliving my childhood all over again because, in a sick sort of way, I had all the same queasy feelings of disappointment, of being left out, that I once had experienced with my father.

I called Guy again. "This is just too hard for me. I don't

even want to live; I can't deal with any of this. Guy, please, just give me something to hold on to."

"Like what?"

The phone slipped from my hand and I vaguely took in the jagged, icy mountain peaks in the distance. There's such untouched beauty in those hills, but I couldn't appreciate it that day. My eyes were so swollen from crying that I don't know how I even saw the road.

It takes about eight or nine hours to drive to my mom's place in Lake Tahoe. I made it in six hours and 45 minutes. I was flying.

I pulled into Skyland, the development in Tahoe where I grew up, comforted by the sentry of lamps lining the entryway. I noticed all the lights were on at my mother's house as I walked up the stairs past the giant, scented pines. Fresh cones the size of small footballs had fallen on the deck, and I pushed one aside with my toe.

"Oh, my God. Are you all right?" my mother asked as she opened the door and scooped me into her arms.

"Mom, he left me," I said, stumbling into the living room and collapsing on the downy white sofa in front of the fireplace.

My mother stood there, arms folded. "What did you do?"

I snapped my head around. She was blaming me for what happened! My mother knew I wasn't easy to be with, and she also knew that I have a fiery temper. She thought of Guy as easygoing, which he was—but not all the time. So she thought I had sparked the separation.

"Thanks a lot, Mom," I said wearily. "You know, I come up here seeking comfort, needing someone to care for me, and the one thing I don't need you to do is judge me."

She looked at me with hurt eyes. "I didn't mean it like that, Tracey."

I said nothing and went upstairs to my old room, slamming the door behind me. I fell across the bed and buried myself in adolescent self-pity.

There was a knock on the door and my mother stood

over me. I didn't turn around. "Are you going to be all right?"

"Yeah, Mom."

"I love you, Tracey."

"Yeah, Mom."

I had no idea what she was saying or what I was saying to her. Nothing meant anything anymore. Not even life. I didn't want to live anymore. I wanted out.

I stayed on the bed for some time in a netherworld—not asleep, not awake—and finally rose to go downstairs to the kitchen. Yes, that's where I wanted to be. The kitchen held all the answers. I walked across the narrow hallway and stood in the doorway of my mother's room, tears falling like rain. "Goodbye, Mom," I whispered. Then I walked by Jeff's room and peeked in. I just wanted to see my little brother. Then I walked downstairs and swept into the kitchen.

Steam billowed from the swimming pool outside the kitchen window, clouding the ebony night. I reached into the counter drawer, pulled out the sharpest knife I could find and sank to the floor. Then, I slashed my wrist. It was unbelievably easy, like slicing into London broil. There was no pain. In fact, there was no blood. I wasn't cut! Then I heard my father's voice: "Get your ass off the floor. Tracey, get up! Trace Face, what are you doing? You can't do this; you're a Davis! You've got to get up! Think of your son!"

I shook my head in disbelief. My head had felt like it was stuffed with cotton candy, but now it felt light and clear. What the hell was I doing? Pop…help me…I knew I had heard my father's voice. He always called me Trace Face. I snapped out of it. My God, what was I thinking? Sam! How could I leave him? How could I have him growing up knowing that his mother killed herself because she couldn't deal with the rough times in life or make her marriage work?

Then I started thinking about all the things I should have recognized from the beginning: If Guy doesn't want me, tough shit, someone else will. If he doesn't need me, I'll be fine. I am a woman and it's time I started acting like one. I have responsibilities to myself and to my child. I'm a mother and I'm going to live and raise my son to be a loving and decent human being. I'm a Davis, and I have to carry my father's torch with pride and honor.

I put the knife in the drawer, listened for a moment to the peaceful silence of the house and went upstairs to bed. I prayed to God to forgive me for being weak and selfish, for thinking only of myself, for not appreciating or understanding how strong I really was. Then I sat, closed my eyes and talked to my father. Once again I needed his forgiveness, and I wanted his spirit to be at ease, knowing his daughter would be all right. The warmth of his love guided me to a tranquil sleep.

The next morning, I told my mother what I had done. She laughed and thought I was kidding.

Driving home that day, I squinted up at the mountains. The sky over Tahoe is so bright, so blue, it almost hurts your eyes. That day, it seemed even more brilliant. A cheerful sky so full of life. I smiled. I felt invincible, like I was back from the dead, which—in a way—I was. I thanked my father for saving me and for giving me strength. The bottom line was, I'm in this marriage…either it works or it doesn't. But no matter what, I'm going to live and I'll be able to survive. I have myself and I have my son.

Guy greeted me at the door when I arrived home. We were both a little cautious. We went to dinner that night and I told him about my suicide attempt. He laughed; he, too, thought I was joking—especially since the knife never cut me. That really hurt. But hey, this was the new Tracey. I actually bounced back, instead of dissolving into tears and making life unbearable for both of us. But our marriage took a little longer to bounce back. Our starting point was Sam. We both loved him and knew he was the linchpin for keeping us together.

We took a trip up to Northern California to see Guy's family and at that time, I was looking to buy a horse. We ended up meeting a family named the Millers in Red Bluff, and bought the horse from them. It was a young horse and we were training him, so we left him there and started driving back and forth.

Tom and Arlene Miller live on a beautiful spread with their son, Judd, his wife, Kim, and their four children: Mandy, Justina, Jadda and Callie. Arlene's sister, Joann, and her husband, Bob, also live there along with Arlene's mother. Each family has a house along the top of a ridge that overlooks acres and acres of beautiful fields and woods, as far as the eye can see.

Tom Miller reminded me so much of my father. He was a man of few words, a very kind man, and he had a way of saying things that made me feel so calm, just as Dad had once we'd really gotten to know each other. The Millers were ranchers, and so honest and close to one another. Everything was pure black and white, no deceptions. Being around them and seeing how a good marriage worked inspired us.

Arlene Miller and I spent hours talking with her daughter-in-law, Kim, about relationships. Guy and I spent countless hours on the ranch with Judd while he made his custom leather products. Even then, Judd took time out from his work to sit and talk about Dad and my family and the rough times we had been through. They probably don't realize they showed me the way back to my sanity.

To know the Millers is to love them. To be loved by them is something altogether special. I needed the Millers, and maybe they sensed that. They showed me what was important in life just by their example. They are such unpretentious, pleasant, real people. Even though they sell the best Arabian Cutters and train all sorts of horses, they are totally down to earth. The Millers are famous in horse circles, and extremely popular. If I live to be 100, I don't think I'll ever meet a group of people as honest, decent and wonderful as the Millers.

Making those eight-hour drives to see the horse gave Guy and me the opportunity to begin to talk to each other. It was the first time Guy ever talked about us, and the process was oddly reminiscent of the talks I had with Dad in Las Vegas that had united us.

Guy told me exactly what he had been feeling: the depression, and how something very important turned out not to be; that he was totally unprepared to go off by himself; that the proverbial grass wasn't greener on the other side. We both realized how much we loved each other and how much we loved Sam. We also realized just how much Dad's illness and death had affected us. Guy also told me that my neediness had become unbearable: the more I needed, the more I repelled him; the more he said no, the needier I became and the less he gave. In our pain and stubbornness, we had just played off each other.

It took him a while to understand why I tried to kill myself. He knew it was a call for attention and help, but I think he finally understood when I explained to him that everything I thought I was, I wasn't. Within a year's time, I had been in an accident that should have killed me, Richard had died in Maddy's arms, I was a new mother, didn't have a job, my father had died and my husband had left me.

Just as it had been with my father and me, Guy and I grew closer through sharing our thoughts. It was that hard—and that simple.

Guy and I slowly readjusted to each other and after a while, we decided to have another child. Our daughter Montana was born on Nov. 8, 1993. We adjusted to Dad's death. But Dad's publicity machine continued to be a well-greased piece of equipment that kept up its relentless momentum even after his death. Any news about his finances, his estate or his show biz legacy was voraciously consumed.

A few months after my father's funeral, reports began to surface that Dad had died a pauper. Lies. Yes, Dad had lived larger than large and had allowed money to glide through his fingers like oil, but he did not leave his family destitute. There may have been some confusion over his outstanding IRS debt, which stood at around $5 million, but his estate— including the house, property, books, antique guns, jewelry and art—was valued between $6 million and $8 million. He left the bulk to Altovise in his will, and he also named her, Mark, Jeff and me as beneficiaries for his insurance policies, which were substantial. Pop had some trust funds for me and my brothers, too.

Mark had problems adjusting to Dad's death and handling the money Dad left him. Mark had been abusing drugs and alcohol for years, but the family hadn't known about it. He was living in Tahoe and partying every night, totally out of control. (Mark went through three wives by the time he was 30.) When he returned to Tahoe after Dad's funeral, he was as devastated by Pop's death as we all had been, but his situation was worse than ever. His drugging eventually caught up to him and he was busted, put on probation and moved with wife number three to Los Angeles. By that time he had gone to rehab, but also had run through his inheritance—and all his friends and family. He was lost. He slipped back to his old habits and disappeared. Mark eventually stopped doing drugs but he was homeless, living on the streets of the San Fernando Valley. Months later, he was walking in Beverly Hills and my mother spotted him while driving by. A friend of Mark's had taken him in. Mark worked on his life and got himself back together and is doing just great today. Dad would be proud.

Pop was ever the clown right up until the last: He stipulated in his will that Shirley Rhodes be given $25,000 just so she could have some "fun," and his pal Clint Eastwood got a gun Gary Cooper had used in one of his Westerns.

As his wife, Alto had to shoulder Dad's tax debt, but she was unable to work out a resolution with the IRS. About a year and a half after he died, an auction was held of what amounted to Dad's memories—his trinkets and toys. It helped pay off part of the tax bill by bringing in close to half a million dollars.

The auction didn't really bother me. Dad had so much stuff, what on earth could you do with all of it? But it was an impressive sale, and it was good to know that Sammy Davis Jr. could still bring 'em in: a pair of his tap shoes went for $11,000; a gold record of "Candy Man" fetched an impressive $4,675; his guest book with signatures from practically every star in Hollywood, the kings and queens of sports and music and anyone else who passed through the house went for over $5,000; a signed picture from Marilyn Monroe, in black and white, sold for $6,050; and one of Dad's outrageous diamond rings (it could break your finger just wearing it) fetched over $30,000. That's my pop!

Then the IRS found more of Pop's memorabilia which Altovise had stashed in a storage room in Burbank. They seized his jukebox, a straw hat, a trumpet, some jewelry and other reminders of Sammy Davis Jr.'s life. Pop believed in indulging himself. If he didn't have a light with him and happened to be in a store that sold 18-carat gold Dunhill lighters, he'd grab one; if he felt like treating 50 friends to dinner, he would. And he spared no expense.

He spoiled me—financially—almost as much as he had spoiled himself. Most of my life, I wanted for nothing. Even in death, Pop made certain that we'd all be provided for. I felt odd about spending the money he left me. I kept thinking it was blood money. At first, I spent a few dollars on little things for Sam, because I knew Pop would want his grandchild to be pampered. But I had a tremendous amount of trouble splurging for me and Guy. I used to talk a lot to my friend Maddy about that because she, too, felt weird about the insurance money from Richard's death.

Maddy and I were good friends; death brought us closer. We could be miserable around each other and understand the natural evolution from shock, anger and pain to guilt, grief and acceptance. She told me I was the only person who could understand because none of her other friends had experienced the loss of someone close. Maddy once called me and said, "It's been a month and I haven't washed the sheets, because if I wash them, the smell of Richard won't be there anymore and I can't deal with it." I knew exactly what she meant, because one day I found a shirt in the closet, one I had worn around Dad before the odor of cancer permeated his sweat glands. There remained a faint whiff of Aramis and I couldn't bring myself to get that shirt cleaned.

I miss my father's fragrance. Oh, yes. I can go into a store and open a bottle of Aramis and smell it. But it's not the same. It hasn't been splashed on Sammy Davis Jr.

And more than his fragrance, I miss him. Very much.

Chapter Nineteen

After Dad's death, the American Cancer Society asked me if I would do some public speaking engagements, and I agreed. I was named head of the Great American Smokeout campaign. Dad had even been a spokesperson at one point. Some joke! He wasn't able to tough it out without smoking.

The Society asked me to go to Sacramento to talk at a black church about smoking and cancer. I accepted without hesitation, but after I made the commitment I got cold feet. I went anyway, and checked into a hotel. A short time later, the bellman delivered a bunch of yellow daffodils and a letter, from a woman whose husband had fought in Vietnam.

She wrote about how her husband had been given a leave from the war and they'd decided to celebrate their wedding anniversary by seeing one of Dad's shows. My father somehow found out who they were—that the husband had been fighting in Vietnam—and he paid their bill that night and gave the woman flowers. She wrote that Dad's show, and his kindness, changed her life. During this terrible period in their lives, he had given them a blessed relief. I still have those daffodils. They were a symbol to me of just how important my father's life had been.

The next day, I went to the church. I had been to only one black church before, the First AME Church in Los

Angeles, for a funeral. I was a Jew. Not only did I feel out of place for that reason, but also because I felt I knew nothing of my black history and culture and that these people would be able to see right through me. *I am a fraud*, I thought. *I'm not even a round peg that doesn't fit in a square hole. I'm not even a peg.* Now I was really nervous. What would I talk about? I had a dopey little speech written, but it seemed so trivial and insignificant. I began to feel sick as I peeked inside the church.

I had been in a separate area with the pastor and his wife, who had beaten cancer years before. She touched me and looked into my eyes. "God bless you, child, for doing this," she said. "I can't believe someone like you would come to a place like this. It's too good to be true."

Someone like me? I thought to myself. *I'm no one. You don't understand—I'm even too scared to go up and speak. I am paralyzed with fear.*

I smiled and thanked her for having me. That's something my parents taught me years ago: You always thank someone for inviting you to something like this because it is an honor and a privilege. Never take it for granted. Somehow, though, I didn't feel worthy. The cancer survivors were arriving. Here I sat, healthy. Lucky, I guess, even though I was mired in a tremendous amount of self-pity.

I ended up talking with a young man who told me he was dying from cancer. He was maybe 18 or 20. Young. He held my hand as he talked to me, perhaps drawing strength from me in some way. "This cancer is killing me," he said. "I don't have that much time. Things like this give me strength."

I looked at him with warmth and support, but my mind was in a tailspin. *Strength? You are dying from cancer. God let you down. Don't you understand? He chose you to get this horrible disease to die by inches and here you are grateful?*

Great, I thought. *I hate God. What has God done for me? He took my dad when I needed him the most. What was that but some kind of cruel hoax: "Hey, Trace, want to have your Dad? Well, too bad, you can't have him 'cause he has to suffer and die.*

And, oh, by the way, he's going to have throat cancer. He's going to be dying while you're pregnant with your first child and you guys will have a wonderful relationship by then, only guess what? You're not going to be able to enjoy it! Sorry! Now, get over it and go on with your life."

What was I doing in this church? None of my prayers had been answered. So how could anyone trust so deeply in the Lord? No matter how hard you pray, things are going to happen a certain way. You get no comfort. No one is going to come in and save the day. Forget it! Give up hope because there is none.

Now the church was full. Choirs from all over had come to compete and sing at the church. There must have been 1,100 people there, all straining to get a look at me, pointing and whispering, "You're famous." "You're Sammy's daughter and we loved him so much. He meant so much to the black community." People came up to me just wanting to stare at me and touch me, to take pictures with me, just as they had when I was a little girl and my dad was still alive. But this was different, this was sweet. I was overwhelmed by the outpouring of love I was receiving from total strangers. And I began once again to feel like a fraud.

I was just about to learn things about my heritage, things daughters learn from their fathers—life things that somewhere down the line make you turn around and say, "Oh, I guess I learned that from my dad." But Dad was dead. This wasn't supposed to happen. What about grandparents taking care of grandkids? Dad changing diapers? Dad had promised me he would beat this thing. We had just found each other. Why?

And then there's Guy. He had told me Pop would be OK. He lied to me. He said Dad's cancer wasn't that bad, and he lied. I hated him for that. I had never needed Guy to be right before and, in my eyes, he let me down. Maybe that's why I punished him so, why our marriage began to crumble. I alternated between needing him so badly that I almost suffocated him, and not wanting him near me at all. Because if he was near me and something happened, I'd be wiped out again.

So here I was in the church, all sorts of isolated thoughts and emotions tumbling about in a fury. Finally, they called my name. I stood up with a dry mouth and went to the pulpit. I was amazed at all the faces I saw.

They had come to see Sammy's Kid. They thought I was like my father. But I didn't feel talented and I didn't know how to get what talent I have out of me to help me through the speech. They were looking up at me, waiting for some sort of impassioned, inspiring talk. But I couldn't find the words. And I had given up the idea of looking at that stupid speech I had taken such pains to write.

Then the words paraded from me as I held firmly to the pulpit: "If you see this shaking, don't be alarmed. We're not having an earthquake. It's just me. I'm extremely nervous." They laughed. Despite myself, I felt at ease. Surely, this was a minor miracle.

I began to speak in earnest, telling the parishioners how my father's death had made me want to hate God. But sitting in this church had helped me realize that it wasn't God I hated. It was the cancer and the cigarettes.

"I was cheated, cheated out of getting to know my father because years of smoking had been more important and more addicting than anything I had known," I said. I saw several heads bobbing in agreement and I knew I was on a roll.

"I look out at you and I see so many beautiful children. If you can't stop smoking for yourself, then stop for those beautiful children. No child should be put in the position that I was put in—wishing and hoping and praying that your father would die. Don't force your children to pray for your death when you can do something so simple to prevent it. Don't you want to see your children's children? My father, Sammy Davis Jr., wanted beyond all else to see his grandson, and he did. But he'll never know the wonders of truly knowing him."

The speech went over very well. People came up to

me afterward, thanking me, with tears in their eyes. I still don't know where the words came from; they just came. But I knew my father was watching over me, and he was proud.

I thought that speech might be a sign that he hadn't left me. But it wasn't. Ever since my father's death I had begged God to give me a sign. I would lie in bed or daydream, squeeze my eyes shut and pray so hard. Anything. Make the wind blow through my window. Make something move. Let me feel something, anything that would let me know that our lives together hadn't ended on May 16, 1990.

I might find a sign at his gravesite, but it took me two years before I could visit Forest Lawn; I couldn't bear the thought of him in the ground. Now I go every now and then and sit beside his grave. It's still a sad journey and a strange one, because that part of the cemetery looks almost like a government monument. There's a huge mural depicting the signing of the Declaration of Independence, and on either side of the mural are two iron gates leading to two separate, small courtyards. You need a key to get in. Dad's headstone lies beneath a spreading tree. There's a marble bench nearby and white marble statues of embracing couples.

I still talk to my father. I tell him how Sam's doing in school and that Montana, my younger child, started walking when she was eight months old. I tell him what's going on with Guy's acting career and our marriage. I tell him about my own achievements as a producer and the vagaries of office politics. Just talking to him out loud helps me sort through difficult decisions.

Each time I go to Forest Lawn, I tell my father, "Thank you. I'm really glad we got to be friends and really got to know each other."

I don't know if I would have been as close to my father if we had had the so-called normal relationship I had yearned for growing up. I didn't want to be "normal" my entire life. That word has frightened me and propelled me to go further, to push. I don't know if having a normal relationship would have allowed us to be as close as we were the last years he was alive. We both fought very hard to have that special relationship. We had to wait a lifetime to get it, but it was worth it.

Before I leave Dad's grave, I always kiss his bronze headstone and tell him how much I love him. Always at that moment, I feel warmth cloak my body.

Ever since I tried to kill myself, I know my father continues to guide me. I heard his voice that night as I ran a knife across my wrist, and it was he who saved my life. I even saw him once, about a year ago. He came to me one night at Mom's house in Tahoe.

I had gone up for a little weekend respite from some problems I was having at work.

That night in my old bedroom, I was stretched across the bed with Montana fast asleep at my side. I was half-awake, half-asleep as my mind kept tunneling in on my office problems. In walked Dad, wearing a V-neck sweater and jeans, like he always had. He didn't have on any shoes, which was odd. I thought I had lost my mind. My heart began to beat faster and I almost panicked. Then a strange calm came over me as he walked over to the bed, and he put his hand on Montana's back.

My father spoke: "Oh, Trace, she is beautiful, isn't she?"

I said, "Yes, Pop. I just wish you had a chance to see her grow up."

He replied, "I will."

I didn't stop for a minute to think about the strangeness of this situation, so happy was I to have my father near me. Somewhere in the back of my mind, a more rational side kept nudging me, telling me I was talking to a ghost and that no one would ever believe me, that I was indeed going crazy.

I started to talk about my problem at work. I told my father I didn't know what to do. He looked at me with a gentle smile and said, "Don't worry about that. Follow your heart. You'll do whatever is best, and it will work out. I trust you."

My throat tightened and I felt tears begin to flood my eyes. "Can you stay, Pop? Please don't leave me. Please stay here with me. Please don't go. Please." I began to sob. I hadn't cried in a very long time and it felt strangely good.

He put his hand on mine and said, "Trace, whenever you need me, I'll be here. I'm not going anywhere. Ever. We fought too hard to get together." He walked out the door as silently as he had entered.

I calmed down and dried my eyes with the sleeve of my sweatshirt. Montana made her little baby noises and slept a peaceful sleep. I felt better about work, but I couldn't comprehend what had just happened. Was I crazy? Was I hallucinating? I truly thought I was slipping toward insanity. I started to panic and called Guy. I couldn't reach him, because he was out riding at the Millers. I stayed awake a while longer, worried about my sanity, before edging to sleep.

I awoke the next day truly shaken. What had happened the night before? Was I losing my mind? I was trembling a bit. Was it a dream? Was it real? I kept going in circles, trying to figure it out. I remember how happy I was with my father's presence and now I was doubting my own sanity.

Later that afternoon, I drove to the Millers to pick up Guy and Sam. I told Guy what had happened, and I could hardly get the words out. "You don't understand, Guy. I'm losing my mind." I started to shake again and told him that maybe I shouldn't be trusted with the children. Guy took my hand and gave it a squeeze. Then he smiled knowingly.

"I don't think you're crazy, Trace," he said. "Things like this happen to people who've lost someone close." His words soothed me a bit, and eased some of my panic.

"You know, you're very lucky, Tracey, lucky to have made that contact," Guy said. "I wish I could have done so with Taryn after she died."

He was right, of course. I was fortunate to have established that bond. I began to understand how the visit from my father gave me confidence, because I no longer was worried about my office problems. My meeting with Dad that night gave me the courage I needed not only for work, but also for everything else I've done ever since.

And I realized that I finally had my sign. I wore the same sweats I had on the night before. I pulled my sleeve up to my face and smelled something wonderful. Aramis. It was the fragrance of my father.

Index

Crystal, Billy, 186-187, 240
Culp, Robert, 163
cult, satanic, 135

D
Daly, Tyne, 195
Damone, Vic, 171
Danza, Tony, 239
Davis, Elvera (Mrs. Sammy
Davis Sr.), 25, 111
Davis, Jeff, adoption of, 47-
48
Davis, Manny, 145-146, 237
Davis, Mark, 45, 46, 47, 49-
50, 57, 183
  adoption of, 40-41, 48
  and death of father, 253
  drug abuse, 138, 253
  health, 87
  marriage to Vesi, 139
  move to Hawaii, 138
  relationship with father,
  138-139
Davis, Sammy, Jr.
  alcohol given up by, 22, 38
  beneficiaries, 252
  Beverly Hills home, 51, 55,
  56, 218, 222, 229
  childhood, 42-43
  children of (see Davis, Jeff;
  Davis, Manny; Davis,
  Mark; Davis, Tracey)
  and cigarette-smoking, 38-
  40, 90, 132, 219, 257, 260
  cooking as hobby, 38, 95-96,
  156
  death, 232, 235-236
  divorce from Britt, 80

  dogs owned by, 74-75
  and drugs, 133-134, 135
  ethnic and racial back
  ground, 25
  funeral, 238-240
  and Garner, 143, 188-189,
  223
  gifts to children, 128, 140,
  143-144
  grandmother, 25
  and grandson Sam, 225-226
  health problems, 119, 141-
  142, 171, 182, 189-190, 196
  hip surgery, 141-142, 171
  at home before death, 217-
  232
  and horseback riding, 69-70
  humanitarian efforts, 203,
  229-230
  IRS debt, 213
  and Judaism, 58-59
  last days, 225-232
  loss of eye in accident, 44
  love of movies, 186
  marriage to Altovise Gore
  (see Gore, Altovise)
  marriage to May Britt. See
  Britt, May
  memorabilia, 253-254
  mother, 25
  movie screenings, 185-186
  personality characteristics,
  43, 92, 94, 121, 128, 141-142,
  185-186, 229-230, 254
  Pickfair purchased by, 80-81
  as prankster, 81
  racism and, 124
  relationship with daughter

Grosvenor House, 98, 100
trips to, 96-100, 101
Luft, Lorna, 195

M
McGuire Sisters, 19, 20
MacLaine, Shirley, 74, 185, 195, 203, 239
McMahon, Ed, 182
Man Called Adam, A, 42
marriages, interracial, 44-45
Martin, Dean, 33, 41, 128, 181, 203, 208, 236
Mastin, Will, 18, 42, 44, 154
Miller family, Red Bluff, 250-251, 263
Minnelli, Liza, 88, 141, 184, 187, 203, 222, 226-227
Monte Carlo, 173-177
"Mr. Bojangles" (song), 17, 43, 93, 182, 239
Murphy, Eddie, 16, 17, 171, 203
"Music of the Night" (song), 175

N
"Name of the Game" (television show), 119
NBC weekly variety show, 41-42
Newley, Anthony, 81
Novak, Kim, 26

O
Ocean's Eleven (film), 20
Odets, Clifford, 41

"One Life to Live" (soap opera), 119

P
Palance, Jack, 82
Paris, 177-178
Peck, Gregory, 182, 183, 184
"Phantom of the Opera" (musical), 175
photographers, 34-35, 51, 214, 236-238
Poitier, Sidney, 182, 183
Ponti, Carlo, 26
Presley, Elvis, 91, 92

R
race, 44-45, 108-109
racism, 27, 51-52, 109, 110-114, 123-126
Rainier family, 174, 175, 176
Princess Caroline, 175-176, 177, 181
Rashad, Ahmad, 95-96
Rat Pack, 58, 61, 80, 185
Ray, Aldo, 244-245
Reed, Andrea, 64
Reed, Donna, 63, 64
Reed, Doran, 64
Reed, Robin, 63-64
Reynolds, Burt, 284
Rhodes, Eygie, 106, 195
Rhodes, George, 89, 93, 100, 209
Rhodes, Shirley, 47, 67, 75, 76, 97, 100, 141, 168, 194, 209, 218, 237, 238, 253
Rickles, Don, 182-183
Robin and the Seven Hoods